A CONTEMPORARY "BLUEPRINT" FOR NORTH ATLANTIC TREATY ORGANIZATION PROVISIONAL RECONSTRUCTION TEAMS IN AFGHANISTAN?

A Monograph

by

Major Andrew M. Roe GH

British Army

School of Advanced Military Studies

United States Army Command and General Staff College

Fort Leavenworth, Kansas

AY 05-06

SCHOOL OF ADVANCED MILITARY STUDIES

MONOGRAPH APPROVAL

Major Andrew M. Roe GH

Title of Monograph: A Contemporary "Blueprint" for North Atlantic Treaty Organization Provisional Reconstruction Teams in Afghanistan?

Approved by:

_____   Monograph Director
Alice Butler-Smith, Ph.D.

_____   Director,
Kevin C.M. Benson, COL, AR   School of Advanced
                                      Military Studies

_____   Director,
Robert F. Baumann, Ph.D.   Graduate Degree
                                      Programs

Abstract

A CONTEMPORARY "BLUEPRINT" FOR NORTH ATLANTIC TREATY ORGANIZATION PROVISIONAL RECONSTRUCTION TEAMS IN AFGHANISTAN? By Major Andrew M. Roe GH, British Army, 66 pages.

The coalition and North Atlantic Treaty Organization (NATO) face a complex and difficult challenge in their search for solutions to the Afghan conundrum. The establishment of Provisional Reconstruction Teams (PRTs) represents a revolutionary step in meeting this challenge. The PRT program combines security and civil action to facilitate regional development. PRTs afford an important interface and make possible information sharing among the local population and government, non-government and international aid organizations. Despite their diminutive size, PRTs possess an innate ability to influence a significant proportion of Afghanistan's rural population, thereby reinforcing regional stability.

Notwithstanding common agendas, significant variances exist between coalition and NATO PRTs. Inconsistencies in *modus operandi*, perceived mandates, roles and responsibilities, national caveats and operational structures have all faced criticism. With international pressure mounting for the International Security Assistance Force (ISAF) to take the lead throughout Afghanistan, this study of existing PRTs is not only timely, but provides a constructive insight for those nations contemplating supporting the reconstruction effort. This investigation is also useful to those nations who staff existing PRTs in the north and northwest and who may be considering transferring their efforts to the southern or southeastern regions; the most insecure and challenging areas of Afghanistan.

This monograph provides a historical overview of Afghanistan's recent history, reviews the contemporary causes of internal instability, illustrates the international response, and analyses three existing approaches to PRTs: those of the United Kingdom, Germany and the United States. It also identifies and evaluates a number of PRT tactical and operational lessons learned. The monograph concludes by combining the pertinent lessons learned into a recommended PRT "blueprint" to meet the contemporary and evolving challenges of provincial security and reconstruction in Afghanistan.

Table of Contents

Table of Figures

Chapter 1

Provisional Reconstruction Teams (PRTs) are an attempt to attack the enemy's (terrorist and anti-government groups) strategic center of gravity -- the allegiance of the Afghan people. By simultaneously providing the Afghan people with tangible humanitarian, reconstruction and security benefits, PRTs build goodwill, trust, credibility and cooperation among the people, the Afghan central government and the coalition forces.

Scott R. Peck, "PRTs: Improving or Undermining the Security for NGOs and PVOs in Afghanistan?"[1]

In November 2002, the U.S. Department of Defense (DoD) announced plans to deploy combined military-civilian Joint Regional Teams (JRTs) to Afghanistan under the command of Combined Joint Task Force - 180 (CJTF - 180). Their role was to stabilize the deteriorating security situation and strengthen the reach of the Transitional Authority of Afghanistan (TAA), without committing an extensive peacekeeping force. JRT secondary roles were: to facilitate reconstruction, to establish favorable working conditions for humanitarian aid workers, and to build a foundation for sustainable post-conflict security.[2] In early 2003, the renamed U.S.-led Provisional Reconstruction Teams (PRTs)[3] were established in Gardez, Bamian and Kunduz provinces.[4] These teams were subsequently reinforced by New Zealand (NZ) and United Kingdom (UK) PRTs.[5] To facilitate cooperation, initial PRT locations were chosen in the same areas where the United Nations Office for the Coordination of Humanitarian Affairs (UNOCHA) established regional offices. The TAA welcomed the PRTs and established a cabinet committee

---

[1] Scott R. Peck. 2004. "PRTs: Improving or Undermining the Security for NGOs and PVOs in Afghanistan?" Joint Military Operations Department, Naval War College, Newport. Page 3.

[2] William B. Taylor. "Testimony," U.S. Congress, Senate, Committee on Foreign Relations, Accelerate Reconstruction in Afghanistan. Washington D.C., 27 January 2004. Internet. Available at: http://www.state.gov/p/sa/rls/rm/28599.htm. Accessed 12 May 2005.

[3] President Hamid Karzai expressed a concern that the name Joint Regional Team implied that the regions had primacy rather than the central government. The name of the teams was subsequently changed to Provisional Reconstruction Teams (PRTs) in January 2003.

[4] The first U.S. PRT was established in Gardez on 31 December 2002.

[5] Work began on the UK PRT in Mazar-e-Sharif province in July 2003.

to provide guidance and support.[6] Following the United Nations Security Council Resolution (UNSCR) 1510, the North Atlantic Treaty Organization (NATO) established a "pilot" PRT under German (GE) leadership in Konduz. By autumn 2004, a total of 19 PRTs were established across Afghanistan.

NATO took command of the International Security Assistance Force (ISAF) in August 2003. ISAF's original mandate was restricted to security assistance within Kabul and its surrounding area. However, UNSCR 1510 authorized a wider security role beyond Kabul. This role took the form of PRTs and temporary military deployments. Subsequently, ISAF took command of the GE PRT on 30 December 2003. Following the NATO Istanbul Summit in June 2004, the two UK-led teams in Mazar-e Sharif (MeS) and Maimana transferred from the coalition to ISAF authority on 1 July 2004.[7] The progressive expansion of NATO PRTs throughout the country is central to NATO's phased four-step counter-clockwise plan to expand ISAF control all through Afghanistan.[8]

Coalition and NATO PRTs successfully introduced a measure of stability to their localities through patrolling, monitoring, influence and mediation. PRTs afford an important interface and facilitate information sharing among the local population and government, non-government and international aid organizations.[9] They have also participated in the reconstruction effort, particularly in areas where other agencies, such as the United Nations (UN),

---

[6] Afghan.com. "The Provincial Reconstruction Team (PRT) in Afghanistan and its Role in Reconstruction." Internet. Available at: http//:light.afgha.com/article.php?sid=33553. Accessed 9 May 2005.

[7] The expulsion of the Provisional Governor, together with the departure of the local militia commander, created a power vacuum that threatened to destabilize Faryab Province. Not wishing to allow a possible standoff between a key regional warlord and the Afghan Transitional Authority, a British PRT was established in Maimana. Its role was to assist the United Nations, the Afghan National Army and the police in increasing the influence of the Afghan Transitional Authority in Faryab Province. The PRT was established five months ahead of NATO's planned schedule

[8] Taken from "Foreign and Commonwealth Office Provincial Reconstruction Teams" webpage. Internet. Available at: http://www fco.gov.uk/servlet/Front?pagename=OpenMarket/Xcelerate/ShowPagee &c=Page&cid=107704746976. Accessed 17 February 2005.

[9] Many parallels can be drawn between the U.S. Army's Province Advisory Teams (PATs) and the U.S. Marine Corps' Civil Aid Program (CAP) in Vietnam, 1965.

have been unable to operate.[10] The PRT has proven to be a strong force multiplier and a way of extending influence throughout the country with economy of effort and resources.

Not all actors agree with the PRTs' stated attributes. Some non-government organizations (NGOs)[11] have labeled PRTs as "security on the cheap" or "war on a budget" and have questioned their ambiguous mandate and legal standing.[12] Representatives of CARE International, for example, have stated, "… the PRTs have neither the resources nor the mandate to engage seriously in either reconstruction or security."[13] Others have expressed concerns that the divide between NGOs and military forces has become increasingly blurred in PRTs, impacting on impartial humanitarian action and raising concerns regarding the personal security of aid workers.[14] Guerrillas routinely target and attack personnel with close relationships with PRTs. They view civilian agencies that are permanently embedded in or routinely support PRTs as instruments of the military and therefore neither independent nor evenhanded. A 2003 Taliban message faxed to the Associated Press warned:

> Our government has always respected the people who are working in NGOs that really want to build Afghanistan. But there is another kind of NGO, which only uses the name NGO but is actually working and spying for the U.S. We advise Taliban all over the country to attack them and extradite [sic] them from Afghanistan.[15]

Other commentators have suggested that PRTs fail to provide a visible presence in the areas where they operate, implying that they are powerless in achieving regional security and

---

[10] The United Nations Assistance Mission to Afghanistan (UNAMA) is mandated by the terms of the Bonn Agreement to carry out an inter-agency coordination function.

[11] NGOs are nonprofit organizations of private citizens usually motivated by humanitarian and/or religious values. The UN recognizes over 40,000 international NGOs. NGOs can be grouped into four types: humanitarian assistance, human rights, civil society and democracy building, and conflict resolution.

[12] The timing of the launch of the PRT plan raised suspicions that the proposal was not only a "second-best" option to the expansion of ISAF but also amounted to a relatively cheap means of keeping a lid on the situation in Afghanistan, while coalition forces and resources moved to Iraq.

[13] Mark Sedra. May/June 2005. "The Provincial Reconstruction Team: The Future of Civil-Military Relations?" Article in *SITREP*, A Publication of the Royal Canadian Military Institute. Official publication of the Royal Canadian Military Institute. Volume 65, Number 3.

[14] NGO/Government Dialogue on Provisional Reconstruction Teams (PRTs) in Afghanistan and the Mobilization of Humanitarian Assistance. 4 December 2003. Internet. Available at: http://www. Peacebuild.ca/whatsnew/PRT-Dialogue-FinalReport.doc. Accessed 20 May 2005

[15] Scott Baldauf. 2003. "Aid Groups in Afghanistan Weigh Good Deeds vs. Safety." *Christian Science Monitor*, 28 October 2003, page 7.

stability.[16] Paul Barker argues in "Why PRTs Aren't the Answer" that the military conducts reconstruction activities poorly. He asserts; "PRTs do not have the time or training to engage communities in a complete and well thought-out development process. The quick-impact, output orientated approach used by PRTs often results in buildings used for purposes other than those intended, wells going idle when pumps inevitably break, irrigation projects being designed to serve the fields of the already rich, and so on."[17]

Conversely, a significant number of informed military and civilian experts argue that the "light footprint" approach to security afforded by a PRT is ideal for Afghanistan; a country with a proven history of dealing violently with perceived occupying forces. Lieutenant General John R. Vines,[18] speaking at Fort Bragg, N.C., on 25 August 2003, described the establishment of the PRTs as "… a stroke of near genius." He stated that they are delivering services that "directly affect the welfare, income and quality of life" of the Afghan people.[19] In many cases, PRTs provide services never before provided by the central government. The European Corps (EUROCORPS) ISAF website adds, "… there is unprecedented breadth of agreement on their [PRTs] necessity and potential to succeed."[20]

Despite common agendas, significant variances exist between coalition and NATO PRTs. Examination of existing training proficiency, structures, national caveats, and methods of operation provides timely information to support decision-making concerning the expansion of NATO's presence in Afghanistan. Such a study could lead to an accepted hybrid or "blueprint" PRT structure for partner or non-partner countries wishing to support NATO's expansion into the

[16] Charlotte Watkins. "PRTs," Chapter 5. Internet. Available at: http://www.institute-for-afghan-studies.org/Contributions/Projects/Watkins-PRTs/chapter5. Accessed 17 February 2005.

[17] Paul Barker. November 3, 2004. "Why PRTs Aren't the Answer." Internet. Available at: http://www.globalpolicy.org/ngos/aid/2004/1103prts.htm. Accessed 17 February 2005.

[18] Lieutenant General John R. Vines commanded coalition forces in Afghanistan from September 2002 to October 2003.

[19] Donna Miles. 21 April 2004. "Terrorist's Can't Compete with Provisional Reconstruction Teams." American Forces Press Service. Internet. Available at: http://www.defenselink mil/news/Apr2004 /n04212004_200404211 html. Accessed 21 October 2004.

[20] ISAF Provisional Reconstruction Teams (PRTs). 17 January 2005. Internet. Available at: http://www.isaf6.eurocorps.org/article.php?article_id=37. Accessed 17 February 2005.

southern or southeastern regions; the most insecure and challenging areas of Afghanistan. In the short term, NATO's expansion into western Afghanistan is confirmed.[21] The Alliance will establish a permanent ISAF presence in the form of four PRTs and one Forward Support Base (FSB). Two existing U.S.-led PRTs will transfer to ISAF control and two new ISAF PRTs will be established, manned by Lithuanian and Spanish troops, respectively.

Monograph Format

The primary question that this monograph investigates is: what are the optimum components of a PRT to meet the contemporary and evolving challenges of provincial security and reconstruction? The question's simple phrasing belies a significant degree of complexity involved in reaching an answer. Thus, there are a number of supplementary questions to address before arriving at a satisfactory answer to the primary research question. Subordinate questions and areas of research include: what are the universal components of success; what are the principal differences between established PRTs; what is the standard of training for personnel deploying to PRTs; what if any, are the impacts of national caveats/limitations; what are the contemporary operational logistic challenges facing PRTs; what are the evolving challenges of PRTs; and what balance of civilian and military assets achieves the greatest effect? The monograph also addresses the current situation in Afghanistan, from both coalition and NATO perspectives.

The scope of this monograph is deliberately narrow so as to make it all the more relevant to the existing challenges faced in Afghanistan. The lessons are covered and presented over five chapters.

Chapter 1 provides an introduction to the PRT concept, states the significance of the subject, establishes the organization of the monograph, overviews the format, and discusses

---

[21] Statement by Secretary General on ISAF Expansion. 10 February 2005. Internet. Available at: http://www reliefweb.int/rw/RWB.NSF/db900SID/JWIN-69HEN5?OpenDocument. Accessed 23 February 2005.

limitations and delimitations. Chapter 2 discusses the warfighting and nation building challenges faced in contemporary Afghanistan. Chapter 3 explains and analyzes the established UK, GE and U.S. PRTs, describes the military/civilian command and control relationship, reviews existing structures, highlights differences in PRT staffing and examines the logistics and security implications of extended lines of communication. Chapter 4 summarizes the lessons learned. Chapter 5 concludes the monograph by recommending changes to the organization and priorities of PRTs, and posits a PRT hybrid or "blueprint" for Afghanistan.

Problem Background and Significance

> What's the first thing in the world you need for anything else to happen, for hospitals to happen, roads to happen, for refugees to come back, for people to be fed and humanitarian workers to come to the country? You've got to have security.
>
> Donald H. Rumsfeld, U.S. Secretary of Defense, 2002[22]

Subsequent to their conventional forces' 2002 defeat, the Taliban and Al Qaida reemerged as an insurgent threat, fighting a low-level guerrilla campaign throughout Afghanistan. Despite coalition efforts, Al Qaida was able to establish new and elusive bases of operation in eastern Afghanistan and western Pakistan. Transformed and determined, both organizations continue to prove capable of independent action in the form of small-scale hit-and-run terrorist attacks and politically motivated assassinations. The coalition's response has been resolute, if not wholly successful; evolving into a low-intensity conflict in Afghanistan and Pakistan to meet the complexities and subtleties of the challenge it faces.[23]

---

[22] Secretary Donald H. Rumsfeld and General Myers, Defense Department Operational Update, 28 March 2002.

[23] Anthony H. Cordesman. 2004. The Ongoing Lessons of Afghanistan: Warfighting, Intelligence, Force Transformation, and Nation Building. Washington D.C., Center for Strategic and International Studies.

At the outset, the coalition failed to "secure" Afghanistan, while tribal factions and warlords were weak. The coalition faces a number of independent armed organizations that rose to fill the power vacuum left by the demise of the organized Taliban. The reemergence of warlords who oversee their territories as independent rulers and only intermittently accept the authority of the central government is of tangible concern.[24] Moreover, the coalition neglected the need for economic aid and an effective reconstruction strategy, relying on NATO and the UN. Both organizations have achieved only marginal success.

The result has been a weak and often ineffective reconstruction effort centered upon Kabul and ISAF.[25] The absence of a strong central government, a poor economy, the dominance of warlords, and the involvement of government or pro-government forces in the drug trade has combined to exacerbate the situation. As a result, Afghanistan has regained its status as the region's largest producer of narcotics.[26]

The coalition and NATO, therefore, face a complex and difficult challenge in their search for solutions to the Afghan conundrum. The establishment of PRTs represents a revolutionary step in meeting this challenge. The PRT program combines security and civil action to facilitate regional development. Unity of command and effort is central. PRTs present a distinct defense against an evolving insurgency in Afghanistan. They possess the ability to influence positively a significant proportion of Afghanistan's rural population, thereby providing regional stability. They deliver services that directly affect welfare, income, and quality of life. Initiatives to repair damaged infrastructure (for example roads, water wells, bridges and schools) have made an important impact on the local population. Such initiatives gain the support and favor of the "broad

---

[24] Farangis Najibullah. "Afghanistan: Disarming the Warlords." Internet. Available at: http://www. Dayafterindia.com/august1/afghan.html. Accessed 29 October 2004.

[25] Draft Department of Defense Directive 9-17-2004 defines reconstruction as, "Efforts by the U.S. Government in coordination with coalition partners and other nations, international organizations, and nongovernmental organizations to create a stable and self-governing polity by establishing the rule of law, rehabilitating the economy, and otherwise improving the welfare of the people.

[26] Jane's Executive Summary, Afghanistan. 2004. Article on-line. Available from: http://www4.janes.com. Internet. Accessed 7 October 2004.

mass of the people," which is central to the long-term stability of Afghanistan and degradation of the Al Qaida and Taliban guerrilla campaign. A mutually supporting network of PRTs will lead to enhanced security over the entire country.

However, NATO has been reluctant to take command of PRTs in the southern and southeastern regions of Afghanistan, arguably the most insecure and challenging regions.[27] With international pressure mounting for ISAF to take a greater lead throughout Afghanistan, a study of existing PRTs is not only timely, but provides a constructive insight for those nations contemplating supporting the reconstruction effort. This study will also prove useful to those nations who staff existing PRTs in the north and northwest and who may be considering transferring their efforts to the south.

Limitations and Delimitations

Limitations are factors that may interfere with the results of a study that the researcher cannot control. A number of limitations shape this study. Although the Combined Arms Research Library (CARL) has a quantity of documents and books regarding Afghanistan and the PRT concept, in general, only limited open source analysis on national approaches is available. Classified information is restricted and therefore generally inaccessible. Furthermore, access to current knowledge about operations in Afghanistan and the security situation is also limited to open source materiel.

Delimitations are the 'who, what, when and where of the study.' They discuss what is included and excluded. A number of delimitations shape the focus of this monograph. This monograph will not investigate in detail the challenging national, multinational and interagency command and control arrangements inherent in PRTs. Nor will this paper discuss the optimum

---

[27] In early December 2005, NATO foreign ministers approved plans to send up to 6,000 troops into southern Afghanistan. The military expansion will take NATO's peacekeeping mission to about 16,000 and make it responsible for security in about three-quarters of the country.

location for a PRT. This study is deliberately limited to looking at three longstanding and

successful approaches to operating a PRT; those of the UK, GE and the U.S. Each is unique.

Chapter 2

Their enmities and bitter struggles spring from the tribal, sub-tribal and regional differences which characterize this, most backward of societies -- differences which escape definition in terms of modern political theory.

Raja Anwar, 1988[28]

Afghanistan is a land-locked country connecting South Asia, Central Asia, and the Middle East. It covers approximately 250,000 square miles and its diverse social community has distinct racial, physical, and linguistic differences. It is a heterogeneous state, in which there are four major ethic groups: Pashtoons, Tajiks, Hazaras, and Uzbeks. The official languages of the country are Pashto and Dari (Afghan Persian). Recent estimates suggest that Afghanistan may have a population of some twenty-six million, divided into some twenty principal ethnic groups and upwards of fifty in total. Islam is the principal religion and is inextricably integrated with local customs. The country has a long tradition of weak and ineffective central government, tribalism, banditry, and ethnic tension. A high percentage of the population lives in remote tribal communities. These groupings are generally isolated and poor, relying on subsistence agriculture and pastoralism. The country's ethnic, religious, and regional diversity result in a wide political fragmentation. Ali Ahmad Jalali argues that Afghanistan evolved as a country composed of autonomous "village states" spread across the entire nation.[29] In some areas, life has continued unchanged for centuries.[30]

---

[28] Martin Ewan. 2001. *Afghanistan: A Short History of Its People and Politics.* London, United Kingdom: HarperCollins Publishers. Page 12.

[29] Ali Ahmad Jalali and Lester W. Grau. 1995. *The Other Side of the Mountain: Mujahideen Tactics in the Soviet-Afghan War.* The United States Marine Corps Studies and Analysis Division, Quantico, Virginia (DFAR 252.227-7020 June 1995). Page xiii.

[30] Andrew M. Roe. 2005. "British Governance of the North-West Frontier (1919 to 1947): A Blueprint for Contemporary Afghanistan?" United States Army Command and General Staff College, Fort Leavenworth, Kansas. Page 42.

The current government of Afghanistan, established under the Bonn Agreement in 2001 to lead the country to free and fair elections, has proven unstable and weak. Ethnic divisions, a perceived over-representation of Tajiks from the Panjshir valley, and a pro-United States policy have greatly reduced the government's authority. Provincial leaders or warlords, many of whom head private armies and possess personal agendas, dominate governance outside Kabul. Legitimate Afghan security institutions are in the early stages of development and are "Kabul centric." The Afghan National Army is embryonic, with recruiting, training and retention proving challenging.[31] Police forces are being "professionalized" under German lead, and Italy is assisting with judicial reforms. In general, progress has been slow.

Modern travel remains limited to a poorly maintained road network linking the major towns and cities. No railroad network exists. Much of the country is overgrazed and there is widespread soil degradation, deforestation and desertification. Formerly a food exporter, Afghanistan now produces less than two-thirds of its own food needs. It is one of the poorest counties in the world and is at the bottom of every economic and social indicator.[32] The country also faces an acute mine and unexploded ordnance problem, a result of Soviet occupation and a subsequent civil war. Its links with international terrorism and its participation in the drug trade, producing seventy percent of the world's supply of opium, are of continued international concern.

Afghanistan's Recent History

If there has been an overriding feature of their history [the Afghans], it is that it has been a history of conflict -- of invasions, battles and sieges, of vendettas, assassinations and massacres, of tribal feuding, dynastic strife and civil war.

---

[31] Jane's Executive Summary, Afghanistan. 2004. Article on-line. Available from http://www4.janes.com. Internet. Accessed 7 October 2004.

[32] Michael E. O'Hanlon and Adriana Lins de Albuquerque. February 23, 2005. "Afghanistan Index: Tracking Variables of Reconstruction and Security in Post-Taliban Afghanistan." Report on line. Available from http://www.brookings.edu/afghanistanindex. Accessed 16 March 2005.

Because of its geographical location, Afghanistan has been on the path of conquest, trade, and migration throughout history. Waves of migrating and warring people have passed through the region. Each has left its imprint on the country adding to the cultural diversity of Afghanistan. Buildings, languages, ethnic groups, cultural complexities, and even religions pay testimony to these influences.

The Afghanistan of today took shape in 1747 under the leadership of Ahmed Shah Durrani. The Durranis exercised power in Afghanistan between 1747 and 1978. By 1842, the empire of Ahmed Shah Durrani began to wane, as the "Great Game" between the Russian and the British Empires played out on the Central Asian chessboard. After an inconclusive British expedition in 1842, Afghanistan lost control of its foreign policy and other powers of state, but was generally left to rule itself. Afghanistan gained full independence after the Third Anglo-Afghan War and Amanullah Khan, who led the war, became king. He began an ambitious reform program, based on a progressive and forward-looking constitution, which granted everyone equal rights. His innovative and radical approach was not universally well received and discontent came to a head in 1928. Amanullah was quickly deposed. After a short interregnum, the Pashtun Nadir Khan took power. Nadir Khan became Nadir Shah, and his son Zahir Shah took over in 1933 and ruled for forty years until 1973. During this period, Afghanistan was a relatively peaceful, moderate and liberal country within the region. The central government matured, providing housing, education, healthcare, and building roads into regions, which had previously been beyond Kabul's control. The Cold War superpowers, the United States and the Soviet Union, provided significant financial assistance.[34]

---

[33] Martin Ewan. 2001. *Afghanistan: A Short History of Its People and Politics.* London, United Kingdom: HarperCollins Publishers. Page 12.

[34] Jeffery Schwerzel. 2004. ISAF Overview. Headquarters ISAF Command Briefing. Kabul, Afghanistan. Page 4.

The period of relative peace and progress came to an abrupt end in 1973 when

Mohammed Daud, a cousin of Zahir Shah, took power in a coup. Daud sympathized with and

supported Marxist factions, which the Soviets had nurtured and trained during the sixties. In

1978, the communists ousted Daud. The imposition of open communist rule resulted in a civil

war, leading to the Soviet invasion in December 1979. For fourteen years from 1978 to 1992,

Afghanistan was under Soviet-sponsored or inspired communist rule.[35]

The Soviet invasion led to greater United States involvement in the region. Over an

eleven-year period (1980 to 1991), the United States and other countries provided the mujahadeen

guerrilla fighters with financial support and arms through Pakistan's intelligence agency.

Additional manpower to fight the Soviets came from Pakistan and the Middle East. In 1984,

Osama bin Laden volunteered to go to Afghanistan. By the end of the decade, he was providing

financial and material support for other Arab-Afghans (this ceased in the early 1990s when he

became disillusioned with the mujahadeen and moved to Sudan). After the Soviet withdrawal in

1989 the mujahadeen continued to fight the Marxist government. During the late 1990s the

Taliban or "religious students" (most of its members had been recruited from the madrassas or

Islamic religious schools) grew in importance. The Taliban "embodied both religious

traditionalism and a Pushtoon tribal ethos, a combination that gave the movement an

exceptionally vigorous dynamic and enabled it to prevail not only against the secular tendencies

in Afghan society, but also against the adherents of an Islamist ideology."[36] Their goal was the

establishment of a strict Islamic state under Sharia law, dominated by the Pushtoons. The Taliban,

with extensive aid from Pakistan, rose to dominate most of the country, but the Northern Alliance

---

[35] Ibid., 5.
[36] Martin Ewan. 2001. *Afghanistan: A Short History of Its People and Politics.* London, United Kingdom: HarperCollins Publishers. Page 226.

(a loose grouping of Pushtoon opponents of the Taliban assisted predominantly by Russia) maintained control over a number of provinces.[37]

Afghanistan, under Taliban rule, became a safe haven for international terrorists, who were able to live, train and plan operations with no restrictions. Most noticeable was the Al Qaida terror network whose leader, Osama bin Laden, returned to Afghanistan in 1996. Inconclusive peace initiatives and fierce fighting between the Taliban and the Northern Alliance dominated the period from 1999 to 2001. Of equal importance to the outside world was a growing humanitarian catastrophe caused by three years of drought.

After the 11 September 2001 terrorist attack on the United States of America, President George W. Bush decided to go to war against Al Qaida and the Taliban under the banner of a global war on terrorism. Special Forces linked up with Northern Alliance commanders and served as advisers and forward air controllers. The first air strikes began on 07 October 2001, 26 days after the terrorists struck. Early combat operations included a mix of air strikes from land-based bombers, carrier-based fighters and Tomahawk cruise missiles launched from both United States and British ships and submarines. The Taliban was a conventional force, fighting in a linear manner. It was readily dismantled from the air. After a relatively brief campaign, the United States-led coalition, working in close cooperation with the Northern Alliance, succeeded in ousting the Taliban regime and chasing the remnants of its fighting forces into the mountains.

The Current Threat

Security in Afghanistan is fragile. Figure 1 depicts the contemporary causes of instability. While considerable efforts have been made to dismantle the Al Qaida network in the southern and eastern areas of the country, progress has been slow and success difficult to quantify.[38] Following

---

[37] Jeffery Schwerzel. 2004. ISAF Overview. Headquarters ISAF Command Briefing. Kabul, Afghanistan. Page 5.

[38] The coalition is also facing a number of evolving guerrilla organizations. The Hezb-e Islami Gulbuddin (HIG), whose stated aim is to fight a jihad or holy war to push the "Americans" out of

the cessation of major combat operations, fighters dispersed among the Afghan population and altered their *modus operandi* to low-level rural insurgency operations.[39] Tribal traditions and a strict adherence to the Islamic faith have made locating and capturing insurgents in remote areas particularly difficult. The strict code of honor called "Pakhtunwali" commands tribesmen to view insurgents as guests, providing protection and shelter. Conversely, Al Qaida and Taliban fighters have threatened tribesmen if they assist the coalition or divulge insurgent locations. Consequently, the coalition has received little intelligence from the tribesmen and achieved few spectacular successes.[40]

Insurgents present a significant threat to security within Afghanistan. They inflicted over 1,000 fatalities between January and August 2004, demonstrating restored confidence and successful reorganization.[41] These attacks were increasingly diverse. As part of a wider intimidation campaign, they targeted Afghan and foreign noncombatants and particularly pro-government individuals or those involved with aid organizations. Besides rural and suburban attacks, guerrilla attacks inside major cities have increased.

Afghanistan and unseat the existing government, is one example that operates in Eastern Afghanistan. Gulbuddin Hikmatyar founded HIG as a faction of the Hizb-I-Islami party in 1977, and it was one of the major mujahedeen groups in the war against the Soviets. HIG has long-established ties with Bin Laden.

[39] The United Kingdom Army Field Manual Volume V, *Operations Other Than War*, Part 1 "The Concept and Practice of Insurgency", defines insurgency as: the actions of a minority group within the state who are intent on forcing political change by means of a mixture of subversion, propaganda and military pressure, aiming to persuade or intimidate the broad mass of the people to accept such a change.

[40] Andrew M. Roe. 2005. "British Governance of the North-West Frontier (1919 to 1947): A Blueprint for Contemporary Afghanistan?" United States Army Command and General Staff College, Fort Leavenworth, Kansas. Page 56.

[41] Jane's Executive Summary, Afghanistan. 2004. Article on-line. Available from http://www4.janes.com. Internet. Accessed 7 October 2004.

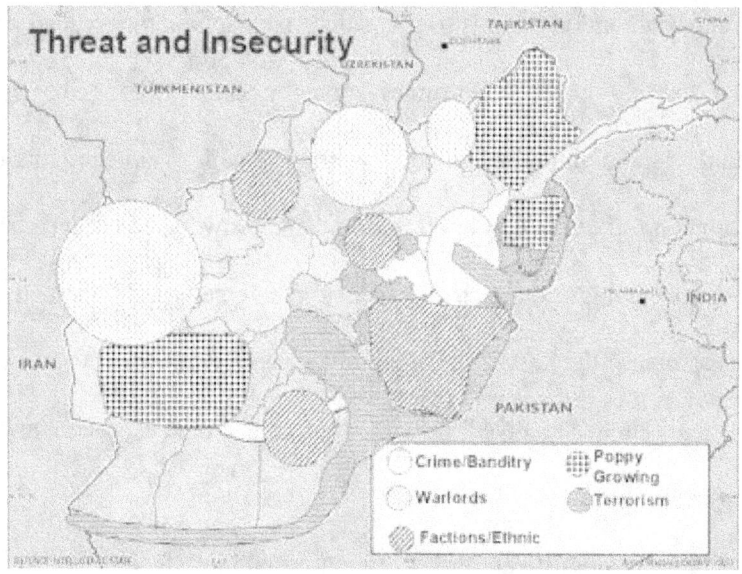

Figure 1. Threat and Insecurity, December 2004.
Source: Headquarters ISAF Command Briefing.

Remnants of Al Qaida and the Taliban rarely gather in significant numbers. A guerrilla force (ambush or raiding party) usually consists of eight to ten fighters. This force is big enough to be hazardous to coalition forces, yet difficult to identify, monitor and intercept prior to an attack.[42] If attackers are met with stiff resistance, they usually scatter and disperse into the local area or population, seemingly without a trace. "Hit-and-run" tactics have been assisted by suicide and car bombings. The attacks are now independent actions. There is no structured coordinating hierarchy or headquarters controlling the insurgency.

A significant number of Al Qaida and Taliban forces have found sanctuary across the border in Pakistan. Insurgents continue cross-border guerrilla warfare from the tribal areas of the North-West Frontier Province in which the Pakistan national government is only able to exercise limited control. Despite some successes in capturing insurgents, United States intelligence analysts believe that new leaders and terrorists may be emerging as quickly as old ones are killed or captured. Furthermore, evidence suggests that Al Qaida may be "subcontracting" smaller

---

[42] Anthony H. Cordesman. 2004. *The Ongoing Lessons of Afghanistan: Warfighting, Intelligence, Force Transformation, and Nation Building.* Washington D.C., Center for Strategic and International Studies. Page 104.

operations to local terrorist groups, providing financial means and training to carry out the attack.[43]

Warlords

Warlords or local commanders present a significant threat to Afghanistan's stability and are a major factor that weakens the central government. They oversee their territories as independent rulers and only intermittently accept the authority of the central government. Once supported and used by the United States in the fight to overthrow the Taliban, these independent powerbases are now viewed as a significant obstacle to centralized control. Coalition support for the warlords has waned and disarmament of their forces is strongly encouraged.[44] The process of "disarmament and demilitarization" is fraught with challenges. Not all warlords wish to deactivate their militias. There are also practical problems regarding soldier reintegration.

Conflict between regional warlords is increasingly common as they compete for influence and territory. Violence is unrestricted since the warlord militias are often far greater in number (10,000-20,000), training and motivation than the government's troops.[45]

Warlords are also heavily involved in the drugs trade. Many of them profit by collecting taxes from local farmers and traffickers transiting territory under their control. Some warlords

---

[43] Ibid., 123.

[44] In 2003 two rival warlords, Mohammed Atta and Abdul Rashid Dostum placed into cantonment areas numerous heavy weapons including tanks, anti-aircraft weapons and rocket launchers. The Mazar-e-Sharif PRT coordinated this action. However, both retained a significant military capability, including armor and artillery.

[45] The major Afghan factions, with their estimated troop strength, warlord, locations and ethnic composition are: (1) Islamic Society, *Jama't-e Islami.* Strength: 15,000 to 25,000. Leadership: Mohammad Fahim Kahn, former National Defense Minister; General Atta Mohammed; Daoud Khan; Bismullah Kahn. Area of influence: Northeast Afghanistan. Ethnic group: mostly Tajik; (2) National Islamic Movement, *Jumbesh-e Melli Islami.* Strength: 6,000 to 8,000. Leadership: Abdul Rashid Dostum (governor of Mazar-e-Sharif). Area of influence: North Afghanistan. Ethnic groups: mostly Uzbek, includes Tajiks, Turkomen, Ismaili and Hazaras; (3) Islamic Unity Party, *Hizb-e Wahdat-e Islami – Khalili.* Strength: Made up of six groups, with a total strength of about 26,000. Leadership: Abdul Karim Khalili; Gul Aga Shirzai (governor of Herat); Ismail Khan (former governor of Kandahar); Hazrat Ali. Areas of influence: Southeast Afghanistan (Ali); Central and Northern Afghanistan (Karim); Northwest Afghanistan (Khan); and West Afghanistan (Shirzai); 4. Islamic Party, Hizb-e Islami. Strength: 100 to 300. Leadership: Yunis Khalis; Burhanuddin Rabbini; Padsha Khan Zadran. Areas of influence: Northwest of Kabul and the Panjshir Valley (Rabbani); Khost, Gardez and Southern Afghanistan (Zadran).

control production facilities and are more deeply involved in the trade as processors and traffickers. The majority use the revenue raised from poppy production as a primary currency for buying weapons and other military supplies.

Drugs

Afghanistan has regained its prewar status as the region's largest producer of drugs. As of June 2004, Afghanistan produced over 75 percent of the world's opium and supplied approximately 90 percent of Europe's heroin. The lack of an effective central government able to implement an anti-drugs program, a poor economic situation and the number of warlords involved in the drugs trade have all combined to worsen the situation. The involvement of government and pro-government forces is disturbing and has been a key feature of the drug trade's development. Initiatives such as the joint Afghan-British plan to destroy 25,000 hectares of poppy fields have made little overall progress.

Opium poppy, with its short harvesting seasons and ability to survive in arid and semi-arid conditions, has proved to be a lucrative crop for many farmers. It is also inextricably linked to their survival. The choice for impoverished farmers is stark; a kilogram of poppy opium commands a price of $80, while the same amount of wheat fetches just seven cents. The absence of traditional economic arrangements, or central control, has encouraged many farmers to grow opium poppy as an alternative "cash crop." Once planted, it requires minimum attention and results in maximum profit. Evidence indicates that warlords and militias have encouraged or forced farmers to shift from traditional styles of farming to poppy cultivation against their wishes.[46]

Britain is the lead country in helping Afghanistan to develop a counter-drug program. It is working alongside the Afghan government to increase law enforcement, improve public

---

[46] Amalendu Misra. 2004. *Afghanistan: The Labyrinth of Violence*. Cambridge, United Kingdom: Polity Press. Page 126.

awareness and promote alternative livelihoods. The U.S., Germany and Japan are also playing roles. For example, Japan donated one-million dollars to support a UN program aimed at treating and rehabilitating drug addicts in three major opium-producing areas: Badakshan, Nangarhar and Kandahar. Despite anti-drug initiatives, progress has been limited. Opium production is forecast to grow over the coming years. The influence of traffickers, traders, producers and processors operating within and outside Afghanistan remains at the core of the crisis. Opium production is a problem that underlies the majority of the issues confronting the stabilization of Afghanistan. There is a growing consensus that victory in the war on terrorism in Afghanistan can only be achieved if the war on drugs is successfully prosecuted.

The Response

Operation Enduring Freedom is the U.S. initial military response to the 11 September 2001 terrorist attacks. Its principal function is conducting combat and counterinsurgency actions[47] against Al Qaida and the Taliban in the southern and eastern areas of the country.[48] The U.S. force has approximately 16,000 soldiers and is augmented by broad coalition support.[49] While operations have been relatively successful, the coalition's pursuit of insurgents is continually hampered by terrain, tribal unwillingness to cooperate and a lack of local knowledge.

NATO is conducting a wholly separate but concurrent reconstruction effort in Kabul and the Northern provinces. NATO's ISAF includes troops from twenty-six NATO, nine partner, and two non-NATO/non-partner countries, but not the U.S. ISAF's mission is to support the

---

[47] The United Kingdom Army Field Manual, *Counter-Insurgency Operations*, defines counterinsurgency operations as: "Those military, paramilitary, political, economic, psychological, and civil actions taken by the government to defeat insurgency."

[48] For example, Operation ANACONDA was one of the largest engagements in the land war. During 02 -18 March 2002, 1,000 troops from the 10th Mountain Division, 101st Airborne Division and United States and coalition special forces, along with 1,000 Afghan troops, secured and searched the Shai-e Kot area of Afghanistan for Taliban and Al Qaida insurgents.

[49] In addition to European and North American support, Pakistan's Army and para-military forces have been engaged in operations against Al Qaida and Taliban insurgents in the North-West Frontier Province and particularly South Waziristan. A total of 1,600 allies from 19 nations support U.S. activities.

government of Afghanistan in building and maintaining a secure and stable environment in order to facilitate the re-building of Afghanistan.[50] The international force continues to be well received by Afghans throughout the capital and has been highly effective at maintaining stability across the city.

NATO has maintained the 6,500-man ISAF in Kabul since 2001 and has declared a wider intent to provide security for the entire country through the establishment of a framework of supporting PRTs. NATO's plan hinges on expanding beyond its success in northern Afghanistan into western Afghanistan, connecting these largely autonomous regions with Kabul, and expanding throughout the entire country thereafter. The expansion has been slow and labored, since nations fail to support the initiative or provide manpower. Many fear that an expansion to remote areas would increase vulnerability to insurgent attacks and create a costly and complex logistics challenge.

Nation Building

Despite the Bush administration's aim of reducing military involvement in so-called nation building activities, deployed forces have become unavoidably engaged in the reconstruction of Afghanistan.[51] Civil affairs personnel have principally coordinated activities, but tactical units have also undertaken self-help initiatives with great success. The PRTs have also played a leading role. In general, these activities have been small-scale projects in areas where the NGO community has difficulty traveling safely to assess and provide aid.

---

[50] Draft Department of Defense Directive 9-17-2004 defines stabilization as, "Efforts by the U.S. Government in coordination with coalition partners and other nations, international organizations, and nongovernmental organizations to create a stable and self-governing polity by establishing the rule of law, rehabilitating the economy, and otherwise improving the welfare of the people."

[51] Even before taking office, members of the Bush team expressed dislike of nation building, suggesting that it was an inappropriate use of United States troops and resources. During the presidential debates, President Bush indicated that he would not have engaged in "nation building" in Haiti, intervened in Rwanda to prevent genocide, or become involved in the Balkans. (Rachel Stohl, "What to do with Afghanistan: Prospects for Stability," *The Defense Monitor*, Volume XXX, Number 9, Page 13).

The Joint-Military Operations Task Force in Bagram is responsible for coordinating humanitarian aid and reconstruction activities throughout Afghanistan. It commands two subordinate Civil-Military Operations Centers at Kharshi Khanabad, Uzbekistan and Bagram, Afghanistan. The task force has nine civil affairs liaison teams. Civil affairs officers and humanitarian workers have deployed together in areas affected by coalition action. This joint deployment is most effective in creating unity of effort. The joint teams have made progress in winning the "hearts and minds" of the tribesmen, by working closely with Afghan villagers and other coalition forces in rebuilding infrastructure (wells, schools, power and water plants). There have been few large-scale projects, though.[52]

Nearly all the principal humanitarian assistance organizations were involved in Afghanistan before the global war on terrorism began. All the key UN agencies, including the United Nations High Commissioner for Refugees (UNHCR), the United Nations Development Program (UNDP) and the Mine Action Service (MAS) had active programs in the country. Hundreds of non-government agencies were also present. These independent and well-meaning organizations continue to assist in the reconstruction of Afghanistan.

Although there have been numerous achievements during the past years, aid for Afghan reconstruction has not been comparable to that for other recent operations. For example, per capita external assistance for the first two years of conflict was $1,390 in Bosnia and $814 in Kosovo but only $52 in Afghanistan.[53] There are also other problems. The growing insecurity for civilian aid workers has reduced their numbers (from January to August 2004, over 40 aid workers were killed and an unknown number wounded), curtailing reconstruction activities

---

[52] Anthony H. Cordesman. 2004. *The Ongoing Lessons of Afghanistan: Warfighting, Intelligence, Force Transformation, and Nation Building.* Washington D.C., The Center for Strategic and International Studies. Page 142.
[53] CARE International in Afghanistan. "Rebuilding Afghanistan: A Little Less Talk, a Lot More Action." Policy brief, October 2002.

outside the security of Kabul.[54] An indication of the complexity of the relationship between military and civilian relief operations was the claim by *Medecins sans Frontières* that the coalition forces were attempting "to link military objectives with the provision of 'humanitarian' assistance" leading to a "confused identity" between the military and aid organizations.

Summary

Afghanistan continues to be a highly unstable country. International intervention notwithstanding, a resurgent guerrilla campaign, the consolidation of warlords in tribal territories and a growing drugs trade present significant threats. All show few signs of abating in the short or mid-term. The government of Afghanistan controls only a small part of the country and has made few inroads into the outlying regions. These areas remain autonomous and only sporadically accept the authority of the central government. The ANA has been slow to evolve and operationally has achieved few successes worthy of note. However, coalition and ISAF nation building efforts throughout the country promise a measure of stability and offer some hope for provisional reconstruction. PRTs appear to be a central ingredient in the recipe for a successful and stable Afghanistan.

---

[54] Jane's Executive Summary, Afghanistan. 2004. Article on-line. Available from http://www4.janes.com. Internet. Accessed 7 October 2004.

Chapter 3

In Gardez, for example, feuding warlords and Taliban-led militants were seen as a major concern, so the PRT deploying to the region placed a high priority on security "presence" and "deterrence" patrols by military personnel, whereas, in more stable areas such as the PRTs located in and around Bagram, the focus has been on reconstruction -- building infrastructure, schools and medical clinics.

Scott Peck, "PRTs: Improving or Undermining the Security of NGOs and PVOs in Afghanistan?"[55]

Coalition and NATO PRTs generally consist of three interrelated functions.[56] The first is the civilian element that facilitates humanitarian aid, reconstruction and development projects. This is the smallest element of any PRT. The second is the military element that stabilizes local security, monitors the security situation and oversees provincial Afghan security forces. The third is the support group, which is comprised predominantly of military personnel. The support group provides logistics, local contracting and linguistic support. "The size and balance of the forces and capabilities of a PRT are directly related to the level of political and institutional sophistication and the level of stability and security of the region in which it will work."[57] Teams working in hazardous areas usually have a larger military force protection element. Lieutenant General David W. Barno, a former commander of the coalition forces in Afghanistan, stated in 2004 that, "There's no cookie-cutter solution for PRTs … one size doesn't fit all."[58] PRTs are frequently supported by individual or formed groupings of multinational military personnel. The

---

[55] Scott R. Peck. 2004. "PRTs: Improving or Undermining the Security for NGOs and PVOs in Afghanistan?" Joint Military Operations Department, Naval War College, Newport. Page 5.
[56] Ibid., 5.
[57] Ibid., 3.
[58] Mark Sedra. May/June 2005. "The Provincial Reconstruction Team: The Future of Civil-Military Relations?" Article in *SITREP*, A Publication of the Royal Canadian Military Institute. Official publication of the Royal Canadian Military Institute. Volume 65, Number 3.

original concept of the PRT stressed the requirement for interagency and multinational representation to support legitimacy.[59]

The overall goal of the PRT concept is to provide a safe and secure environment, allowing the political and reconstruction processes the space and time required to achieve progress.[60] However, because PRTs are small, lightly armed and located in isolated regions, it is often impractical for military personnel to enforce peace in the area in which they operate. This has been a major criticism of many PRTs.[61] Security is routinely -- and almost exclusively -- achieved through liaison and dialogue. Established relationships are used to "defuse" developing or potential problems.[62] PRTs rely on maintaining a significant measure of consent at the local level. Outbreaks of violence are frequently left unchecked, since PRTs are relatively powerless to intervene in inter-militia fighting. In more hostile environments, PRT personnel often only provide local area security for NGO reconstruction activities.

Some suggest that PRTs must play a wider role beyond physical security. "A PRT is really a catalyst. It forms a focal point in a particular area, with the goal of building not only relationships but also serving as an accelerator in the rebuilding of the nation and extending the reach of the Afghan central government."[63] Unfortunately, a number of NGOs want PRTs to exclusively fulfill a security role in the regions that they operate, reestablishing the divide between NGOs and military forces.

---

[59] NGOs will be fully represented, or, if they remain independent, at least be linked for coordination, flexibility and efficiency.

[60] "A safe and secure environment is one in which the population are confident that they are able to live and work, educate their children and take part in legitimate political debate without the fear of intimidation and violence. Such a condition allows NGOs and other experts to carry out their work in confidence and safety." Source: Russell N. Wardle. 2004. "The Search for Stability: Provincial Reconstruction Teams in Afghanistan." U.S. Army War College Barracks, Pennsylvania. Page 6.

[61] Charlotte Watkins. "PRTs," Chapter 4. Internet. Available at: http://www.institute-for-afghan-studies.org/Contributions/Projects/Watkins-PRTs/chapter4. Accessed 17 February 2005.

[62] The final recourse is the PRT's ability to "reach back" for reinforcements, air strikes or other assistance.

[63] U.S. Department of Defense. "Special Department of Defense Briefing on Provincial Reconstruction Teams in Afghanistan." Internet. Available at: http://www.defenselink mil/transcripts /2004/tr20040217-0446.html. Accessed 25 January 2005.

The addition of the word "reconstruction" into the PRT title in 2003 caused added anxiety amongst the NGO community, some of whom believe that PRTs represent the politicization of aid.[64] NGOs have continued to stress their own overarching requirement for impartiality, neutrality and independence. Their concerns are well founded. "A further blurring of the line, from the NGO perspective, occurs when NGOs participate in village assessments with uniformed PRT Civil Affairs personnel and when Special Operations Forces personnel attempt to integrate with the local population in civilian clothing."[65] It is clear that PRTs must do more than just routine security duties in the areas in which they operate, but the concerns of the NGO community have to be taken into account. This is occurring, and some PRTs have evolved considerably over the last two years, often learning from their mistakes. In addition, Headquarters ISAF has developed structurally to support the growing number of PRTs under its authority. The establishment of a PRT coordination cell in 2004, commanded by a one-star British general, has assisted with unity of effort and information sharing. It is also at the planning forefront of ISAF's expansion throughout Afghanistan.

This chapter analyzes three existing approaches to PRTs; those of the UK, GE and the U.S. The UK PRT has been at Mazar-e-Sharif (MeS) since 2003. The PRT was originally under coalition control but subsequently transferred to ISAF authority in 2004. The GE PRT at Konduz was originally a NATO "pilot" PRT. With a change in the NATO command structure, the Konduz PRT transferred to ISAF control in December 2003. Both the UK and GE PRTs operate in the relatively benign northern region, where insurgent activity has ended. By contrast, a number of U.S. PRTs[66] conduct reconstruction activities in the south and southeast where

---

[64] The Peace Operations Working Group of the Canadian Peace-building Coordinating Committee suggests that PRTs should be renamed to correctly reflect their mandate. They propose using the title "ISAF Security Support Team" (ISST). Source: NGO/Government Dialogue on Provincial Reconstruction Teams (PRTs) in Afghanistan and the Militarization of Humanitarian Assistance. Available at: http://www.peacebuild.ca/whatsnew/PRT-Dialogue-Final/Report.doc. Accessed 15 June 2005.
[65] Scott. R. Peck. 2004. "PRTs: Improving or Undermining The Security for NGOs and PVOs in Afghanistan?" Joint Military Operations Department, Naval War College, Newport. Page 12.
[66] Kandahar, Khowst, Gardez, Jalalabad.

coalition combat actions continue. These PRTs require a greater focus on force protection. Reviewing ISAF and coalition PRTs should allow the unique and common components of success to be identified.

UK PRT -- Mazar-e-Sharif

A functional breakdown of the UK PRT at MeS, as of October 2004, is shown at Figure 2. The PRT is commanded by a colonel[67] and has a senior representative from the United States Department of State (DOS), the United Kingdom Foreign and Commonwealth Office (FCO), the UK Department for International Development (DFID) and the United States Agency for International Development (USAID). Civilians serve in the PRT for two years, providing continuity and experience. They ensure that the aid organizations are used effectively and are integrated into the civilian-led assistance coordination program. The PRT has a UK budget of approximately $1.5 million for development and reconstruction programs.[68] Significant additional funding is provided by USAID. While the principal focus of the civilian element of the PRT is reconstruction, the military element has placed particular emphasis on restoring local government infrastructure, in addition to security activities.[69] Security sector reform, support to institution building, and the encouragement of economic development have been identified as principal priorities.[70] A clear delineation exists between the military, development and political components. Reconstruction and development programs remain subordinate to DFID's authority with minimal military involvement in either their identification or implementation.

---

[67] UK PRT commanders are post battalion command. All possess extensive operational experience and are handpicked for the appointment. PRT commanders come from combat, combat support and combat service support backgrounds.

[68] Charlotte Watkins. "PRTs," Chapter 4. Internet. Available at: http://www.institute-for-afghan-studies.org/Contributions/Projects/Watkins-PRTs/chapter4. Accessed 17 February 2005.

[69] The PRT's mission is to, "Set the conditions for the achievement of stability within the PRT AO in order to strengthen the Islamic Transitional Government of Afghanistan's influence and marginalize the Afghan regional causes of instability." Source: Mazar-e-Sharif Command Briefing.

[70] Security Sector Reform is a lead-nation approach to rebuilding Afghanistan as a sovereign state. The five pillars of the strategy are: establishing the Afghan National Army (U.S.); establishing the judiciary system (Italy); establishing law enforcement agencies (GE); disarming, demobilizing, and reintegrating the Afghan Militia Forces into society (Japan); and counter-narcotics (UK).

MeS PRT faces command and control challenges. While the PRT reports directly to headquarters ISAF in Kabul, it also answers to a second national reporting chain to the Permanent Joint Headquarters in the UK. Additionally, the PRT reports to both the British Embassy and Headquarters British Forces in Kabul as well as the FCO and DFID in London. The command and control arrangements are complex but effective.

The PRT's area of responsibility is vast and diverse, covering four provinces. The region is home to two opposing warlords.[71] Both guarantee PRT security and permit access to the tribesmen and their families. Despite occasional flare-ups, the region is relatively benign and peaceful. Military Observation Teams (MOT), using civilian cross-country vehicles to conduct routine patrols and monitoring activities, are assigned to each province.[72] Patrols are highly visible and concentrate on both low and high-risk areas. A dedicated intelligence cell, manned by trained intelligence personnel, provides MOT guidance. Figure 3 shows a MOT traversing difficult roads in Balkhab Province. MOTs provide stability to the region by brokering local ceasefires, overseeing disarmament programs and supervising the cantonment of heavy weapons. MOTs have developed close working relationships with regional leaders and warlords. They have also overseen Afghan National Army (ANA) operations, providing a quality control function, when units deploy to the MeS PRT area of responsibility. Each region patrolled by a MOT contains a "safe house" for overnight accommodation. These are guarded by members of the local militia for a small fee. MOTs routinely wear berets and carry side-arms. Patrols often deploy for upwards of five days. Deployed MOTs maintain contact with PRT headquarters by satellite communications.

---

[71] Mohammed Atta and Abdul Rashid Dostum.

[72] Each UK MOT consists of a Liaison Officer (captain), an Assistant Liaison Officer (sergeant-warrant officer), a driver (private soldier), and an interpreter (locally employed civilian). The MOT is supported by an additional driver (private soldier), an escort (lance corporal) and a combat medical technician (who also doubles as a second escort).

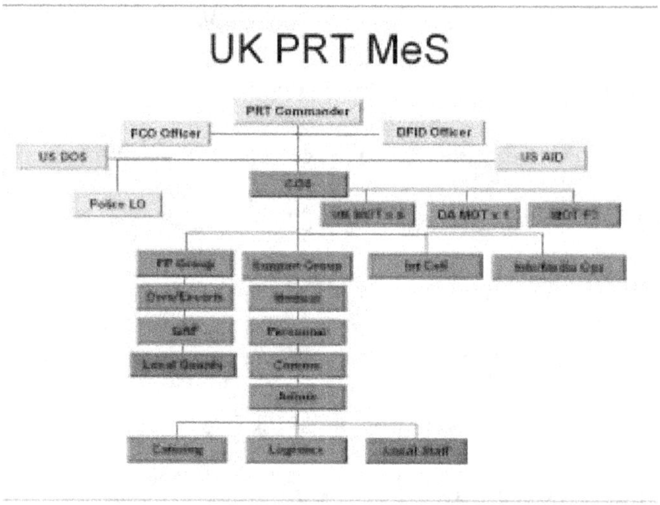

UK PRT MeS

Figure 2. Functional Breakdown of Mazar-e-Sharif (MeS) Provisional Reconstruction Team, June 2004. Source: Mazar-e-Sharif Command Briefing.

The internal Force Protection Group (FPG) maintains a dedicated Quick Reaction Force (QRF) and provides routine base security at MeS. A second line "northern region QRF" is located at MeS airfield. This is a reinforced UK company of two rifle platoons and a support weapons platoon. The support weapon platoon has a section each of mortars, anti-tank weapons and medium machine guns.[73] Local guards provide PRT gate control during daylight hours. Air support from the coalition is available on call for serious breaches of security or for demonstration purposes. A comprehensive Support Group includes a reinforced medical section, with a doctor and dentist (but no large animal veterinarian), as well as a dedicated logistics support team. The PRT also includes a police liaison officer, whose responsibility it is to coordinate efforts to train and equip local police. The UK PRT model is tailored to the needs of the northern region.

The core of the PRT is comprised of a regular infantry company[74] that rotates every six months.[75] The short duration of UK tours has been criticized. Rigid personnel rotation schedules

---

[73] *The Green Howards' Gazette.* The Regimental Magazine of The Green Howards (Alexandra, Princess of Wales's Own Yorkshire Regiment). August 2004, Volume CXII, Number 1074, Page 12. United Kingdom, Method Publishing.

[74] Recent peacekeeping experiences -- including Northern Ireland, Bosnia and Kosovo -- have all had a significant impact on the British approach to employing experienced regular soldiers.

have resulted in a lack of institutional memory at MeS. The infantry company commander, a major, fills the role of the Chief of Staff (COS) and company soldiers fill the ranks of the MOTs, FPG and QRF. Senior captains fill the role of liaison officers. Experienced warrant officers or color sergeants act as their deputies. Additional headquarters company soldiers -- with special logistics skills -- reinforce the support group. Personnel from the Intelligence Corps man the intelligence cell. A small number of females support the team, but they rarely accompany MOTS. The PRT comprises about 130 personnel, including multinational personnel from Denmark, Sweden, Lithuania and Romania.[76]

Gurkha infantry soldiers have been successfully employed at MeS on two separate occasions.[77] They bring unique capabilities to the PRT. Gurkhas are readily accepted in the localities in which they work and enjoy a cultural understanding of the people and the environment. They also speak many of the local languages, negating the requirement for an interpreter to support a patrol. Gurkhas understand the humanitarian needs of the people. They recognize the requirement for measured and deliberate reconstruction activities based on their experience in Nepal.[78] Gurkhas have proved invaluable in advising the civilian element of the PRT.

Training for PRT employment is extensive and based on a proven technique developed for units deploying on six-month emergency tours in Northern Ireland. Initial emphasis is placed on individual training and basic skills, before transitioning to team and mission specific

---

[75] In contrast, the New Zealand Defense Force (NZDF) personnel who man the New Zealand PRT at Bamyan are drawn from all three services and serve for 12 months.

[76] "Foreign and Commonwealth Office Provincial Reconstruction Teams." Internet. Available at: http://www.fco.gov.uk/servlet/Front?/pagename=OpenMarket/Xcelerate/ShowPage&c=Page&cid=107704 746976. Accessed 17 February 2005.

[77] Gurkhas are British Army soldiers who are recruited in Nepal. A government-to-government arrangement between Nepal and Great Britian allows the Gurkhas to swear allegiance to Britian's monarchs while retaining Nepalese citizenship. The only restriction Nepal places on their service is that they cannot be sent into battle against other Hindus -- a prohibition that does not apply to combat against Al Qaida and the Taliban.

[78] Large-scale western initiatives or uncoordinated local projects have the potential to rapidly change -- or undermine -- the fabric of remote and fragile communities, leading to instability.

proficiency. The UK Operational Training and Advisory Group (OPTAG) coordinates all instruction, with additional support from in-theater advisors. Training lasts for up to four months and is regularly reviewed and updated. Particular emphasis is placed on cultural awareness, driving skills and basic language training. MOTs receive specialist training in satellite communications and mediation.[79] Throughout the training period, all personnel receive regular operational and intelligence updates.

Figure 3. UK MOT Patrol Through the Balkhab Province of Northern Afghanistan.
Source: Mazar-e-Sharif Command Briefing.

In support of the ISAF mission to establish a network of PRTs across Afghanistan, the UK established a Forward Support Base (FSB) at MeS airfield in June 2004. The FSB is staffed by personnel from the UK, GE, Sweden and Norway, supported by elements of the ANA. This fixed deployment provides a dedicated QRF of company strength and addresses logistical support for all PRTs in the region under ISAF authority. The QRF is trained to deploy by a variety of land and air assets, which include civilian cross-country vehicles based at the FSB, UK C130 transport

---

[79] *The Green Howards' Gazette.* The Regimental Magazine of The Green Howards (Alexandra, Princess of Wales's Own Yorkshire Regiment. August 2004, Volume CXII, Number 1074, Page 11-13. United Kingdom, Method Publishing.

aircraft based in Kabul and GE CH-53 helicopters based in Termez, Uzbekistan. The QRF has been proactive in its duties. The company routinely undertakes a busy rotation of patrols across the nine Northern provinces, which comprise ISAF Area North.[80] The FSB has proved invaluable in re-supplying isolated PRTs at extended lines of communication.

GE PRT -- Konduz

A functional breakdown of the GE PRT at Konduz is shown at Figure 4.[81] A colonel from the German Ministry of Defense (MOD) and a senior diplomat from the Ministry of Foreign Affairs (MFA) "jointly" control the PRT. Additional civilians from the Ministry of Economic Cooperation and Development (MECD) and the Ministry of the Interior (MOI) are also members of the PRT.[82] "The representatives of these different ministries perform tasks according to a clear-cut division of labor.[83] The representative of the MFA, in his function as civilian head of the PRT, coordinates the work of the personnel provided by MECD and MOI, whereas the task of the military component -- together with the indigenous security forces -- is to ensure a safe environment and thus provide the conditions for the support and reconstruction work of the GE and international aid organizations."[84] Civilians serve in the PRT for six-month tours, mirroring their military counterparts. Centralized coordination is essential to prevent duplication of effort and to ensure complementary strategies are pursued in a synchronized manner. The commander of the Kunduz PRT has overall military responsibility for the GE PRT Group, including the GE

---

[80] *The Green Howards' Gazette.* The Regimental Magazine of The Green Howards (Alexandra, Princess of Wales's Own Yorkshire Regiment. December 2004, Volume CXII, Number 1075, Page 9. United Kingdom, Method Publishing.

[81] GE took over responsibility of the U.S. PRT at Konduz in late October 2003.

[82] The MOI representative is a senior GE policeman.

[83] The civilian mission is to, "Support and promote reconstruction in the four Northeastern provinces with GE financial and material means." Emphasis is placed on strengthening the authority of the central government and promoting political-administrative structures.

[84] The German PRT Group. Internet. Available at: http://www.isaf6.eurocorps.org/prt.php?prt =kunduz. Accessed 14 February 2005.

PRT at Feyzabad.[85] A country information advisor (FAS), a public information officer (PIO) and a provost marshal (PM) directly support the command group. The PM also commands the military police (MP) platoon. The FAS and PIO are experienced reserve officers.

The Konduz PRT faces command and control challenges similar to those of the UK PRT in MeS. The PRT reports directly to Headquarters ISAF in Kabul and -- through a second national reporting chain -- to the German Operations Command in Germany. Additionally, the PRT reports to the GE Embassy and Headquarters GE Forces in Kabul, as well as the MFA, MECD and MOI.

The PRT's geographical area of responsibility is considerable, covering the provinces of Konduz and Takhar. To cover effectively Takhar, the PRT operates a "safe house" in Taloqan, the provincial capital. A second GE PRT at Feyzabad covers the province of Badakhshan, and the Dutch PRT at Pol-e Khomri patrols the province of Baghlan. PRT Konduz centrally coordinates all locations and activities. To date, the region has been relatively quiet.[86] General Daoud, the only noteworthy warlord in the region, has remained supportive of the PRT's reconstruction efforts and the government of Afghanistan.

PRT Konduz consists largely of a headquarters with a sustaining headquarters support element, a protection/patrols element and a medical company. The headquarters element has a dedicated staff formed from the full range of military disciplines, and is coordinated by the chief of staff, a lieutenant colonel. The protection/patrols element provides the Liaison Monitoring Teams (LMTs). LMTs provide a security/reconnaissance/assessment function similar to the UK MOTs. LMTs deploy in three-vehicle wheeled armored convoys. The vehicles are military and are clearly marked to distinguish them from NGO vehicles. The patrol size is mission dependant,

---

[85] In October 2004, a second GE PRT was activated at Feyzabad. Its geographical area of responsibility is the province of Badakhshan.

[86] There have been a number of isolated incidents. For example, a remote-controlled mine exploded in June 2004 as a GE patrol passed by, killing at least two children and two Afghan men. "Attack Raises Questions Over German Presence in Konduz." Internet. Available at: http://www.dw-world.de/dw/article/0,1238505,00 html. Accessed 23 February 2005.

but is generally in the region of 12 soldiers. Patrols always include a human intelligence specialist as well as a trained medic and tactical air controller. Local Afghan guards support patrols. LMTs routinely wear berets and carry side arms for personal protection. The protection/patrols element also includes a dedicated QRF platoon. The QRF is equipped with armored light-track vehicles called Wiesels.[87] These are rarely used but remain a potent deterrent and capability.

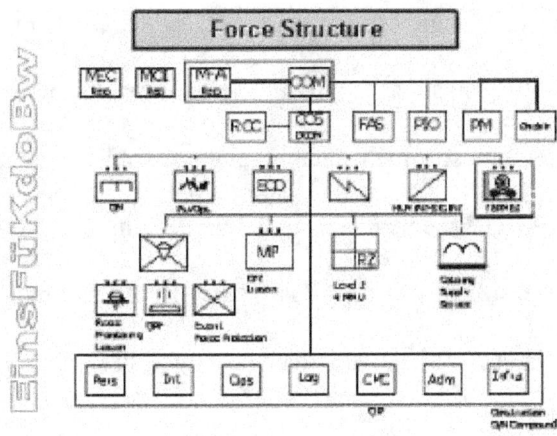

Figure 4. Functional Breakdown of Kunduz Provisional Reconstruction Team.
Source: Konduz Command Briefing.

The PRT contains a number of capability-specific elements. These include: a psychological operations (PsyOps) platoon, an explosive ordinance disposal (EOD) platoon, a signals platoon and a human/signals intelligence (HUMINT-SIGINT) platoon. The chief of staff coordinates the work of these elements. Additional capabilities can be accessed through electronic "reach back" to Germany. Troops routinely deploy to the PRT for six-month tours. Under a Federal German Parliament mandate, up to 450 soldiers can be employed in northern Afghanistan. This provides the PRT military commander the opportunity to surge or withdraw forces depending on the threat. The "personnel pull principal" provides the contingent

---

[87] The Wiesel is an armored light-tracked vehicle developed by the German company Rheinmetall Landsysteme. It is air-portable and can be carried inside a GE CH-53 helicopter. The Wiesel is armed with a 20 mm cannon.

commander a high degree of flexibility. In general, 260 GE soldiers and 20 civilians are employed in Konduz.[88]

The GE government has placed a number of explicit caveats on the Konduz PRT. GE personnel are prohibited from supporting direct action counter-terrorism or counter-narcotic operations.[89] Patrols must use GE Army armored cross-country vehicles, despite the increasingly benign security situation. Outsourcing of services within the local community is also strictly controlled. In addition, a level 2 medical facility occupies valuable space within the PRT compound, in order to meet imposed medical constraints. A soldier wounded in action must be evacuated to a recognized level 2 medical facility within 90 minutes of injury.[90] Such national and NATO standards have resulted in offers of assistance from other nations being turned down. Clear rules define the levels of certified competency required to support GE soldiers on operations.

Germany signed a bilateral agreement in 2003 with Uzbekistan to establish a national FSB at Termez, close to the Afghan border, to support the GE Contingent (GECON) in Afghanistan. Termez offers a runway capable of supporting commercial aircraft and is home to the GE fleet of CH-53 helicopters. Termez proved invaluable for PRT Konduz in the initial stages. Some of the functions undertaken by Termez are now occurring from the FSB at MeS.

GE troops deploying to the Konduz PRT are well prepared. Formed units and individuals are warned for operations twelve months in advance of their deployment. Preparation is gradual

---

[88] The German PRT Group. Internet. Available at: http://www.isaf6.eurocorps.org/prt.php?prt =kunduz. Accessed 14 February 2005.

[89] ISAF and U.S. PRTs are also prohibited from supporting direct counter-narcotic operations. " PRTs are not involved in counter-narcotics -- period … folks have been very emphatic that PRTs, in order to maintain the support of the Afghan people, cannot be seen to be involved in eradication." Source: Thomas Donnelly and Vance Serchuk. "Nation Building, After All." 4 April 2005. Internet. Available at: http://www.aei.org/publications/filter.all,pubID.22246/pub_detail.asp. Accessed 8 June 2005.

[90] A level 2 medical facility conveys a major advantage. There are always an abundance of trained medics available to support routine patrols. Medics often conduct local clinics to assist tribesmen and their families.

and mission orientated.[91] Military personnel regularly train with civilian reconstruction experts and cultural advisors. Particular emphasis is placed on cultural awareness and basic language training. Key leaders attend a regular program of operational updates.

U.S. PRTs

Combined Joint Task Force - 76 is the coalition operational headquarters in Afghanistan and has responsibility for a number of task forces.[92] Two Combined Task Forces (CTF) have PRT responsibilities. CTF - Bronco covers the south and southeast of Afghanistan and is responsible for PRTs in Kandahar, Lashkar Gah, Qalat and Tarin Kowt. CTF - Thunder covers the central and eastern region of the country and is responsible for PRTs in Asadabad, Bamian (under New Zealand command), Gardez, Ghazni, Jalalabad, Khowst, Parwan, and Sharona.

U.S. PRTs are commanded by a regular or reserve lieutenant colonel and include senior representatives from USAID, the Department of State and the United States Department of Agriculture.[93] Senior civil service equivalents from the Afghan Ministry of the Interior routinely support U.S. PRTs. They are often inadequately trained and require authority from Kabul before supporting regional reconstruction initiatives. Many are former Afghan generals with little experience in regional reform. United States Justice Department police trainers and Drug Enforcement Agency representatives reinforce teams for counter-drug efforts on request.[94] Such specialized support is often limited in duration. Permanent U.S. civilians serve in the PRT from 12 to 24 months, providing stability and much needed local knowledge.

---

[91] Lieutenant General Hans-Otto Budde, Chief of Staff of the German Army, stated during a presentation to the United States Army Command and General Staff College on 16 September 2005 that, "All training [in the German Army] is operationally focused." He also emphasized the importance of placing the mission first in pre-deployment training.

[92] CJTF - 180 changed in mid-April 2004 to the 25th Infantry Division (Light), resulting in a designator change to CJTF - 76.

[93] Occasionally, U.S. PRTs are commanded by Colonels, or, in one case, a Navy Reserve Commander.

[94] U.S. Department of Defense. "Special Department of Defense Briefing on Provincial Reconstruction Teams in Afghanistan. Available at: http://www.defenselink.mil/transcripts/2004/tr 20040217-0446.html. Accessed 25 January 2005.

PRT commanders have been appointed from all four services. No specific skill set or experience level is required. Despite the predominantly male dominated character of Afghanistan, both male and female commanders have proven successful. Commanders serve in the PRT for 12 months and have considerable autonomy in allocating financial support. PRT commanders can approve small-scale reconstruction activities up to $25,000. For larger projects up to $150,000, brigade commander approval is required. For major reconstruction projects, USAID is often the lead agency. In 2003, U.S.-led PRTs had a financial allocation of approximately $12 million set aside for small-scale programs.[95]

U.S. PRTs do not possess dedicated MOTs or LMTs. Civil Affairs soldiers trained in medicine, psychology, engineering, and law conduct area-wide assessment patrols, following a structured program.[96] While carefully focused, these patrols are infrequent in terms of regularity. Patrols, which can last up to 5 days, identify priority needs through liaison with district and provincial leaders. U.S. PRTs make use of Afghan regional structures to determine reconstruction efforts. Patrols, however, have faced considerable criticism.

> My own observations bear witness to predominantly male and often heavily armed U.S. Civil Affairs Officers conducting assessments by meeting with village leaders over a two or three hour period. As far as I could gather, there was no crosschecking of data to determine the reliability of the information, or to identify the needs of women, ethnic minorities, or other groups with particular needs. Projects were then selected using raw data, with no apparent analysis of underlying social, economic or political factors, or with an eye to the future sustainability of projects.[97]

---

[95] Charlotte Watkins. "PRTs," Chapter 4. Internet. Available at: http://www.institute-for-afghan-studies.org/Contributions/Projects/Watkins-PRTs/chapter4. Accessed 17 February 2005.

[96] Civil Affairs teams are responsible for conducting village assessments (in collaboration with NGOs, the UNAMA and Afghan government officials) to determine the reconstruction needs of communities. "In addition, the teams monitor the progress of reconstruction projects and hire and manage local contractors and laborers to undertake reconstruction projects whenever possible. The PRT Civil Affairs teams provide job and economic opportunities for the Afghan people, impart a sense of ownership in the reconstruction process and instill faith in the central government." Scott. R. Peck. 2004. "PRTs: Improving or Undermining The Security for NGOs and PVOs in Afghanistan?" Joint Military Operations Department, Naval War College, Newport.

[97] Charlotte Watkins. "PRTs," Chapter 4. Internet. Available at: http://www.institute-for-afghan-studies.org/Contributions/Projects/Watkins-PRTs/chapter4. Accessed 17 February 2005.

Human intelligence specialists routinely support assessment patrols. Personnel conducting liaison duties wear soft hats and carry side arms for personal protection. Civil Affairs patrols are reinforced by infantry soldiers for protection. The size of the protection element is dependant upon the threat, but is routinely 8-10 soldiers in strength. Soldiers employed on protection duties wear helmet and body armor.

Patrols in benign areas routinely use civilian cross-country vehicles. Those in hostile regions use up-armored military vehicles (U.S. Army HUMVEES) to meet force protection regulations. If an overnight stay is required, patrols occupy village buildings constructed or renovated with U.S. funding. Schools and warehouses are frequently used. These contain the basic facilities required by a patrol and meet acceptable sanitary standards. Local Afghan police, who conduct high visibility mobile and foot patrols, regularly provide outer security. Internal security is the responsibility of the protection element. Patrols operating in remote areas request local advice to identify appropriate accommodation. If no suitable lodging is found, patrols move to remote locations to establish temporary overnight shelter and protection. In addition to routine patrols, some U.S. PRTs have undertaken local police reform, providing supplies and training.[98] While not clearly mandated to undertake such activities, many commanders see these activities as essential to enforce regional security.

The infantry company is the largest element of the PRT. Companies can be regular Army or mobilized from the National Guard. Both have proved effective. A number of National Guard companies have served multiple deployments in Afghanistan and contain experienced soldiers, some with prior PRT experience. Soldiers serve in the PRT for 12 months, rotating between patrolling and security duties. Infantry companies maintain a robust capacity to defend the PRT. This is especially true of those PRTs deployed within hostile territory. For instance, the PRT at

---

[98] For example the Ghazni PRT. Source: Thomas Donnelly and Vance Serchuk. "Nation Building, After All." 4 April 2005. Internet. Available at: http://www.aei.org/publications/filter.all,pubID. 22246/pub_detail.asp. Accessed 8 June 2005.

Gardez is reinforced with a heavy weapons platoon for perimeter security.[99] Routine patrols use a squad of infantry as a dedicated quick reaction force. Some U.S. PRTs employ an additional protection force formed from local Afghans. This force has proved to be extremely effective and is relatively inexpensive to maintain. Local Afghans often provide perimeter security and formed subunits frequently accompany assessment patrols, providing much needed local knowledge.

The support element is the second largest component. It provides logistics, communication, linguistic, personnel and medical support. Medics often accompany patrols. However, for focused medical support to villages, Civil Affairs personnel can request tailored medical teams. Medical teams include both male and female doctors, as well as dentists and large animal veterinarians.[100] These have proved to be a great success, despite a lack of female interpreters. The Civil Affairs section is small. It consists of between 8-10 specialists, including an officer. Many are reservists with extensive experience in their field of expertise. PRTs sometimes contain a small Military Police team for local law enforcement training and assessment.

The strength of a U.S. PRT in a benign area, such as Herat, is approximately 80 personnel. Some commentators suggest this figure is too small when compared to NATO PRTs and have also raised concerns over team compositions. Scott Peck argues; "Most U.S.-led PRTs … have insufficient military and civilian staffs to accomplish their objectives. Instead of the percentage of civilian staff increasing in the PRTs as the conditions improve in the province, they

---

[99] Afghan.com. "The Provincial Reconstruction Team (PRT) in Afghanistan and its Role in Reconstruction." Internet. Available at: http//:light.afgha.com/article.php?sid=33553. Accessed 9 May 2005.

[100] "Coalition veterinarian personnel traveled to the Nangalam village near Asadabad firebase from 8-10 November 2003 and performed veterinary services as part of the coalition's civil military efforts. 153 goats, sheep, and cattle were treated on the first day, and 226 goats, sheep and cattle were treated on the second day … the veterinarians performed a much need preventive medical service ..." Source: GlobalSecurity.org. Internet. Available at: http://www.globalsecurity.org/military/world/afghanistan. Accessed 11 July 2005.

have decreased."[101] This criticism has some merit. Many civilian agencies are incapable of providing additional personnel to PRTs and are already overstretched meeting the basic requirement. Military specialists, such as Civil Affairs personnel and Military Police units, face similar problems. To compound the problem, the U.S. Secretary of Defense stated in early 2004 that he wanted U.S. troops withdrawn from PRTs as quickly as feasible.[102]

U.S. PRTs working in south and southeastern Afghanistan operate similarly to those in benign areas. However, patrols are increased in size and strength depending on the threat. Fifteen vehicle patrols are not uncommon. Personnel wear helmets and body armor. Patrols are heavily armed and mounted in four-wheel-drive up-armored vehicles. Formed units of the ANA routinely support patrols. Overnight stays are rare due to the threat. PRTs are often restricted to certain areas. For example, the U.S. PRT in Kandahar operates only within the perimeter of Kandahar city. A battalion-size task force conducts operations outside the city due to the threat. PRT activities are routinely dovetailed with wider coalition activities to provide additional depth and security. PRTs are often collocated with coalition and ANA forces in a Forward Operating Base (FOB). While such an approach has many force protection and command and control (C2) benefits, there are concerns regarding the distinction between troops operating from the same location conducting counterinsurgency operations and reconstruction activities in the same province. Some PRTs have taken this a step further. The U.S. PRT in Laghman Province shares an operations room with coalition forces to synchronize provincial activities. This confers many benefits when planning and synchronizing operations.

U.S. PRTs operating in high threat environments face distinctive national command and logistic challenges. PRTs often work alongside regular combat arms battalions conducting counterinsurgency activities. High-impact operations often have a damaging effect on PRT

---

[101] Scott. R. Peck. 2004. "PRTs: Improving or Undermining The Security for NGOs and PVOs in Afghanistan?" Joint Military Operations Department, Naval War College, Newport. Page 16.
[102] Vince Crawley. 2004. "Rumsfeld Wants Soldiers Off Afghanistan Rebuilding Teams," *Army Times* 64, number 34. Pages 32-33.

initiatives. Conflict results from the requirement to balance necessary counterinsurgency operations with focused reconstruction activities. Disagreements frequently occur between PRT and battalion commanders on local policy. Resolution is achieved through dialogue and personal relationships. Colonel Russell N. Wardle OBE argues in "The Search for Stability: Provisional Reconstruction in Afghanistan" that; "In practical terms, it is difficult to see coalition forces subordinated to a PRT and therefore a robust coordination mechanism needs to be in place."[103] U.S. PRTs also face routine manning and logistical challenges. PRTs are often undermanned and routinely filled with inexperienced soldiers from reserve or National Guard units. They are also rated as a second priority for logistic and administration support, so PRT commanders often have to fight for basic resources. PRTs are viewed as poor relations to the regular combat arms battalions.

U.S. PRTs have faced recent criticism in three specific areas. Firstly, personnel employed on PRT duties are often inadequately trained. Pre-deployment preparation is generally theater orientated but not mission specific. Ad hoc groups, many of whom are reservists or National Guard, conduct individual training, but little emphasis is placed on team proficiency. Deployed personnel often find themselves ill prepared for the unique challenges faced by PRTs operating in remote areas. Continuation or refresher training, once in theater, is almost non-existent. Major Joseph F. Monroe USMC argues in "Afghanistan: Security Integration and Organization" that:

> A comprehensive training program for incoming [PRT] personnel is a must. This training cannot be a three-day "hand wave" of current issues. The training should include a brief history of insurgency/counterinsurgency/security operations, successes and failures, and lessons learned. Culture and Afghan history should be tailored to the province the soldier will operate in. Along with language training, cultural training should make up the majority of the training program.[104]

---

[103] Russell N. Wardle. 2004. "The Search for Stability: Provincial Reconstruction Teams in Afghanistan." U.S. Army War College Barracks, Pennsylvania. Page 9.

[104] Joseph F. Monroe. 2004. "Afghanistan: Security Integration and Organization." Naval War College, Newport.

Secondly, U.S. PRTs have placed a heavy emphasis on implementing small-scale, quick impact development projects[105] that have made only limited impact on the provinces they support.[106] A number of projects have subsequently proved to be a duplication of effort with NGO initiatives. Others have often resulted in initiatives being used for purposes other than those intended. Finally, U.S. PRTs have been criticized for the use of aid conditionality. As an example, a U.S. PRT in Zabul Province distributed leaflets that threatened to stop aid if tribesmen did not provide useful intelligence. This initiative was discontinued due to public criticism.[107]

Summary

PRTs symbolize a unique solution to the complexity of achieving regional stability in Afghanistan. UK, GE and U.S. PRTs have demonstrated that the goals of NGOs and the military are not totally incompatible as many would argue. However, significant hurdles remain. The ambiguous role of PRTs has overlapped appreciably with the mandates of civilian aid organizations, drawing considerable criticism and practical concern. PRTs have been inconsistent in addressing local governance and judicial reform. There are also internal conflicts with units conducting counterinsurgency or counter-drug operations. These often have a harmful effect on PRT initiatives and require careful coordination to achieve unity of effort. Few PRTs have embraced civilianization in order to help restore the perception of normality. Moreover, PRTs have not transitioned to local government "ownership" and are still not seen as an extension of the central government. Internally, PRTs face national caveats, manning constraints and civilian-military composition challenges. Each presents a unique challenge.

---

[105] Mark Sedra. May/June 2005. "The Provincial Reconstruction Team: The Future of Civil-Military Relations?" Article in *SITREP*, A Publication of the Royal Canadian Military Institute. Official publication of the Royal Canadian Military Institute. Volume 65, Number 3.
[106] Quick impact assistance projects have some advantages. They win friends quickly and can garner valuable information about the guerrillas as a result.
[107] Mark Sedra. May/June 2005. "The Provincial Reconstruction Team: The Future of Civil-Military Relations?" Article in *SITREP*, A Publication of the Royal Canadian Military Institute. Official publication of the Royal Canadian Military Institute. Volume 65, Number 3.

Chapter 4

> As sweeping as the reconstruction needs are, it is important that the goals remain
> largely restorational. Efforts at profound transformation will meet resistance
> based in Afghanistan's traditional culture. Assistance must also foster
> institutional capacity and not merely flow to projects that suit donor needs but in
> the process disrupt the local economy.
>
> Larry Goodson, "Afghanistan's Long Road to Reconstruction," 2003[108]

Analysis of established coalition and ISAF PRTs in chapter 3 has identified a number of

tactical lessons learned, many of which necessitate Table of Organization and Equipment (TOE)

changes to existing national structures. These are: more female soldiers and interpreters should be

employed in liaison patrols to address women's needs; specialist capabilities, such as

psychological operations personnel, explosive ordnance experts, information operations and

human/signals intelligence personnel should be incorporated into PRT establishments; PRT

deployments to more insecure regions in Afghanistan will require a substantially larger and more

robustly equipped security force; routine and high visibility liaison patrols serve as a significant

deterrent to local hostility and factional tension and must occur in greater frequency in areas of

high threat; PRTs must receive adequate resourcing and support to achieve their mandate, and;

since "institutional memory" is routinely threatened by six-month UK and GE troop rotations,

personnel with liaison duties should have an increased tour duration. However, this analysis has

also identified ten operational lessons/areas of concern for further deliberation. These present a

more pressing challenge for policy makers and planners tasked with extending ISAF's reach.

---

[108] Larry Goodson. 2003. "Afghanistan's Long Road to Reconstruction." *Journal of Democracy*, Volume 14, Number 1 (January 2003), pages 82-99.

Lessons Learned/Areas of Concern

> Flexibility was a key aspect of the PRTs' effectiveness, but at times flexibility seemed to be a euphemism for ambiguity.
>
> Michael J. McNerney, "Stabilization and Reconstruction in Afghanistan: Are PRTs a Model or a Muddle?"[109]

Coalition and ISAF PRTs lack a unified mission and agreed approach for establishing the conditions to achieve regional stability.[110] Unity of effort is threatened and potentially will become increasingly disjointed as ISAF expands into the south and southeast of Afghanistan. Each PRT possesses its own mission and focus and is subject to unique national expectations. For example, the UK PRT at MeS focuses principally on security sector reform, support to institution building, and encouragement of economic development. In contrast, the GE PRT emphasizes security and stability through confidence-building measures, support to the Disarmament, Demobilization and Reintegration (DDR) process and security sector reform.[111] U.S. PRTs focus largely on "quick impact" development projects, averaging fifty to one hundred and fifty thousand dollars per project.[112] Moreover, civilian humanitarian aid, reconstruction and development projects are routinely executed by national bodies within PRTs (for example, FCO, DFID, MFA), without regional or nationwide coordination with NGOs, which is essential to prevent duplication of effort.[113] To implement this coordination may prove challenging.

---

[109] Michael J. McNerney, "Stabilization and Reconstruction in Afghanistan: Are PRTs a Model or a Muddle?" *Parameters*, U.S. Army War College Quarterly, Volume XXXV, Number 4, Winter 2005-06, page 36.

[110] Scott. R. Peck. 2004. "PRTs: Improving or Undermining The Security for NGOs and PVOs in Afghanistan?" Joint Military Operations Department, Naval War College, Newport. Page 4.

[111] Disarmament, Demobilization and Reintegration (DDR) is the process whereby the militia forces are disarmed, their units demobilized, and they are reintegrated as productive members of Afghan society. Japan is the lead nation for DDR although the program is designed and executed by the United Nations Assistance Mission in Afghanistan (UNAMA).

[112] Mark Sedra. May/June 2005. "The Provincial Reconstruction Team: The Future of Civil-Military Relations?" Article in *SITREP*, A Publication of the Royal Canadian Military Institute. Official publication of the Royal Canadian Military Institute. Volume 65, Number 3.

[113] Scott R. Peck. 2004. "PRTs: Improving or Undermining the Security for NGOs and PVOs in Afghanistan?" Joint Military Operations Department, Naval War College, Newport. Page 14.

Although nobody is in principle against coordination, in practice efforts to achieve coordinated action lead to irritation and frustration. Coordination efforts can quickly provoke institutional "turf" wars ... Or to quote the popular saying amongst humanitarian practitioners -- "everybody wants coordination but nobody wants to be coordinated."[114]

While the establishment of the PRT Coordination Cell in 2004 has gone some way to harmonize national military approaches, its primary mission has been coordinating ISAF's expansion. Little effort has been made to synchronize coalition and ISAF PRTs within a unified civilian and military framework, adhering to an agreed strategy, executing a unified mission. The result has been competing missions, individual approaches and occasionally, primacy of national agendas.

The ambiguous mandates of coalition and ISAF PRTs demand greater clarity to support unity of effort.[115] A 2003 Agency Coordinating Body for Afghan Relief policy brief warned:

To date, NGOs know of no legal framework authorizing the work of the PRTs or any transparent reporting mechanism through which accountability for PRT actions can be achieved or PRTs' success measured. There is neither a documented agreement with Afghan administration nor terms of reference that clearly articulate the PRTs' purpose, mandate, and legal accountability; nor has reference been made to the PRTs' responsibilities under international law.[116]

To support unity of effort -- and even in the absence of clear mandates -- proven approaches should be implemented nationwide, taking into consideration subtle regional and provincial differences. For example, in addition to providing regional security and establishing favorable working conditions for humanitarian aid workers, PRTs should focus on the rehabilitation of local government infrastructure.[117] Emphasis should be placed on training and

---

[114] Charlotte Watkins. "PRTs," Chapter 2. Internet. Available at: http://www.institute-for-afghan-studies.org/Contributions/Projects/Watkins-PRTs/chapter2. Quote Kühne in Ottunu and Doyle, 2001. Pages 141 and 387. Accessed 17 February 2005.

[115] PRTs have an ambiguous mandate under Operation ENDURING FREEDOM. They are not traditional peacekeeping operations. They do not have a Chapter VI or a Chapter VII mandate under the UN Charter.

[116] ABCAR Policy Brief. 16 January 2003. "NGO Position Paper Concerning the Provisional Reconstruction Teams." Internet. Available at http://www.careusa.org/newsroom/specialreports/afghanistan/01152003_ngorec.pdf. Accessed 01 August 2005.

[117] "The PRTs should exploit their comparative advantage by directing their resources to security rather than reconstruction activities. The presence of a PRT, while largely symbolic, will serve as a powerful deterrent to violence and factional tension." Mark Sedra. May/June 2005. "The Provincial

equipping local police forces as well as helping to reform the penal and judicial systems; areas that have been neglected by some PRTs.[118] Regional security is essential and local police will increasingly replace the coalition and ISAF security forces conducting such duties. The challenge is considerable.

> The police station, which boasted four permanent policemen, a mud hut and a very angry guard dog, was in the middle of nowhere. Lieutenant Subar [MOT Juliet commander, MeS PRT] was surprised to find a new policeman in charge of the isolated post and he listened intently as he was told that the previous police chief was accused of illegally "taxing" herdsmen, beating up locals and demolishing a family's home so he could steal their roof timbers.[119]

Regional police training programs are but one example of an initiative that has been successfully undertaken by UK and U.S. PRTs without a clear mandate. PRTs should also assist with the restoration and provision of equipment for government offices and facilities, particularly in remote districts. The reestablishment of a functioning local administration is a central component of regional stability. It also assists in extending the authority of the government of Afghanistan. However, military elements of PRTs should avoid physical reconstruction activities and providing routine humanitarian assistance.[120] The employment of U.S. Civil Affairs personnel on such duties has been the subject of considerable criticism, especially regarding the "blurring" of the divide between NGOs and military forces. NGOs are better structured and trained to conduct reconstruction and humanitarian activities. The civilian element of the PRT should continue to be the principal means of facilitating provincial reconstruction and development projects through information sharing. Critically, PRTs must be divorced from offensive counterinsurgency operations. Even sharing base locations creates unnecessary

---

Reconstruction Team: The Future of Civil-Military Relations?" Quote from *SITREP*, A Publication of the Royal Canadian Military Institute. Official publication of the Royal Canadian Military Institute. Volume 65, Number 3.

[118] Russell N. Wardle. 2004. "The Search for Stability: Provincial Reconstruction Teams in Afghanistan." U.S. Army War College Barracks, Pennsylvania. Page 12.

[119] Graham Diggines. 2005. Gurkha Road Trip. *Soldier*, Magazine of the British Army. June 2005, Volume 61/06.

[120] PRTs must be capable of providing humanitarian assistance in emergency situations or when called upon to do so by the international community. Failure to do so would lead to considerable (and unwanted) criticism in times of crisis.

confusion in the eyes of the local population. Mark Sedra cautions in *SITREP* that; "It has become clear over the past three years that the goals of Operation ENDURING FREEDOM and that of the wider Afghan reconstruction process can be incompatible."[121]

PRTs should be "civilianized" and "Afghanized"[122] wherever possible, in order to help restore the perception of normalcy and return the military to its primary mission. Unfortunately, the percentage of civilian staff has not increased in the PRTs as the security situation has improved. Indeed, in some PRTs the number has fallen.[123] Many civilian agencies are unable to provide additional personnel to PRTs and are already overstretched meeting the basic requirement. The inclusion of representatives from the Afghan Ministry of the Interior is a welcome step in the process, but further initiatives are required. For example, qualified local Afghans or graduates from the Civil Service Academy in Kabul should be incorporated into key PRT appointments.[124] This would help with perceived legitimacy and is a natural evolution of the PRT concept. Moreover, regular units of the ANA should perform routine liaison patrols, monitoring activities and security duties, replacing coalition or ISAF soldiers. Trained ANA officers and soldiers are well suited to developing working relationships with warlords and overseeing disarmament programs. Incorporating civilian and military Afghan elements into the PRTs is a prudent step towards a midterm exit strategy and should be encouraged. It also affords local communities a feeling of "ownership" over their PRTs.

The establishment of a dedicated intelligence cell within each PRT may prove beneficial in countering the insurgency and coordinating operations. Regional intelligence has been almost

---

[121] Mark Sedra. May/June 2005. "The Provincial Reconstruction Team: The Future of Civil-Military Relations?" Article in *SITREP*, A Publication of the Royal Canadian Military Institute. Official publication of the Royal Canadian Military Institute. Volume 65, Number 3.

[122] Scott. R. Peck. 2004. "PRTs: Improving or Undermining The Security for NGOs and PVOs in Afghanistan?" Joint Military Operations Department, Naval War College, Newport. Page 16.

[123] Afghan.com. "The Provincial Reconstruction Team (PRT) in Afghanistan and its Role in Reconstruction." Internet. Available at: http//:light.afgha.com/article.php?sid=33553. Accessed 9 May 2005.

[124] United Nations Development Program - Afghanistan webpage. Internet. Available at: http://www.undp.org.af/about_us/overview_undp_afg/sbgs/prj_csc.htm. Accessed 26 September 2005.

nonexistent and established PRTs have been disinclined to establish intelligence cells or to share information. PRTs have used small numbers of human intelligence personnel to great effect on routine patrols. These specialists have been particularly effective in major centers of population such as Konduz and MeS. The employment of such personnel, especially those with language skills, should be expanded to all liaison patrols/activities. Moreover, linking and exchanging intelligence in a coordinated manner may lead to progress in dismantling the Al Qaida and Taliban network. This is a central role that headquarters ISAF is ideally placed and structured to coordinate once PRTs have established an intelligence function. Additionally, a dedicated intelligence cell within each PRT could also provide information for the counter-drugs program. While "PRTs are not involved in counter narcotics -- period,"[125] intelligence cells could provide direction to law enforcement and eradication activities without PRTs becoming directly involved.[126]

PRTs should also develop closer working relationships with regional leaders and warlords. Military liaison officers or qualified civilians should be assigned to work with these leaders, monitoring activities and providing a mentoring function. UK liaison patrols at MeS have been particularly effective in this area working with Mohammed Atta and Rashid Dostum. The presence of liaison officers has deterred the outbreak of large-scale factional clashes and enhanced regional stability. Liaison officers should be trained in the procedures of local governance and possess sufficient authority to act on behalf of the PRT commander. Staff-trained lieutenant colonels or qualified civilians are ideally suited to fill this role. In extremis, experienced captains have proven adequate.

---

[125] Quote from Colonel Randy Brooks, a Canadian reservist responsible for overseeing PRTs in Kabul. Source: Thomas Donnelly and Vance Serchuk. "Nation Building, After All." 4 April 2005. Internet. Available at: http://www.aei.org/publications/filter.all,pubID.22246/pub_detail.asp. Accessed 8 June 2005.
[126] Nations have been emphatic that PRTs, in order to maintain the support of the Afghan people, cannot be seen to be involved in poppy field eradication.

Attention should also be given to maximizing and reinforcing embedded medical support to the local population. Most PRTs include a doctor, dentist and a number of highly trained medical technicians. As the majority of the rural areas influenced by the PRTs lack the infrastructure to meet the basic health care needs of the population, medical assistance is an important factor in securing the "middle ground." Each PRT should be reinforced with a female doctor as well as a number of female medical interpreters and a large animal veterinarian. Female healthcare and veterinarian support to working animals have been critical areas neglected by some PRTs. For more focused medical support to villages, tailored medical teams should be formed. These have been used to great effect by U.S PRTs, but not by ISAF. ISAF resources could be pooled to meet such a requirement on a case-by-case basis with prior notice.

Nations committing personnel to PRTs must give serious thought to training prior to and during deployment. The unique role and remote location of PRTs calls for structured and progressive training. Individual preparation is essential, but comprehensive team and mission specific training must follow. Instruction is best undertaken in formed role-specific teams. Such a model has proved successful for both UK and GE personnel undergoing pre-deployment training. The U.S. has adopted a more generic approach, focusing predominantly on individual and theater specific training. This approach has some significant shortcomings -- especially the lack of team and mission specific training -- and is not recommended. Training emphasis should be placed on cultural awareness, driving skills, peace building and basic language training, in addition to vehicle anti-ambush drills. Patrol personnel must receive specialist training in satellite communications, mediation, first-line trauma care and close air support. Training should be supervised and regularly updated by personnel with recent PRT experience. Moreover, all personnel should receive frequent operational and intelligence updates specific to the area in which they will operate. Training must continue once in theater to maintain proficiency levels. Opportunities for training must be created and test exercises routinely undertaken.

Consideration should also be given to the selection of military personnel working in PRTs. Reservist and National Guard soldiers have been routinely employed in U.S. PRTs, even in key appointments. UK and GE PRTs have relied almost exclusively on highly trained regular soldiers. Regular soldiers confer many benefits. They often have previous operational experience and are already formed and trained in established structures.[127] Their level of training proficiency is generally higher than that of their reservist or National Guard counterparts and they are immediately available without the requirement for lengthy mobilization. Paul Parker states in "Why PRTs Aren't the Answer" that:

> PRTs draw heavily on the skills and experience of reservists who -- while full of the best intentions -- do not have a strong understanding of development best practice, and have limited knowledge of local languages and culture.[128]

However, skilled reservists can be used to great effect in PRTs. For example, the GE PRT employs a country information advisor and public information officer, both of whom are experienced reservists whose civilian employment reflects the role they fulfill while on active duty. While there are some advantages to employing reservists or National Guard soldiers in PRTs, a preponderance of regular soldiers is suggested as the optimum solution for success.

PRT military commanders must be carefully selected. Previous operational experience, a record of accomplishment of successful command and useful skills/education should all be key attributes taken into account during the selection process. Colonel William A. Rigby proposes in "Nation Building: An Essential Army Task" that:

> The environment today and tomorrow requires leaders who can effectively work in an interagency process, who understand the myriad requirements and complexities inherent in developing stable societies from instability. The types of skills or background … include: language proficiency; backgrounds in civic or

---

[127] Routine squad and platoon formations can be directly transferred into many PRT structures maintaining established cohesion.

[128] Paul Barker. November 3, 2004. "Why PRTs Aren't the Answer." Internet. Available at: http://www.globalpolicy.org/ngos/aid/2004/1103prts.htm. Accessed 17 February 2005.

governmental functions such as city management ... and experience working with other interagency partners.[129]

It is also advised that male commanders are more preferable than female due to the overtly male-dominated nature of Afghan culture. However, in extremis, female commanders have proved successful.[130] PRT commanders should hold the rank of colonel. This allows PRT commanders to outrank the regular combat arms battalion commander working in the same geographical area, providing a greater emphasis on reconstruction activities. It also permits international parity, ensuring coalition and NATO PRT commanders are of the same rank. Like all personnel employed within the PRT, commanders must be carefully trained for their role. Comprehensive training as well as short attachments to established PRTs is recommended. Commanders must also understand the nature and role of each of the civilian elements employed in the PRTs. Pre-deployment education in this area is especially important and may necessitate attachments or briefings from those civilian elements represented in the PRT.

The coalition should consider establishing two separate command structures in Afghanistan; counterinsurgency and reconstruction. Combined Joint Task Force - 76 should command both centrally. Such an initiative would help address the existing friction between high impact counterinsurgency operations and gradual reconstruction activities. Subordinating PRTs to combat formations has proven ineffective and counterproductive. Reconstruction efforts have been marginalized and PRTs under resourced.[131] Establishing a dedicated chain of command for PRTs confers many potential benefits. A centralized command authority could have responsibility for overseeing pre-deployment training, ensuring appropriate PRT manning, synchronizing

---

[129] William A. Rigby. 2003. "Nation Building: An Essential Army Task." U.S. Army War College, Carlisle Barracks, Pennsylvania.

[130] Conversely, the employment of female commanders supports the U.S. policy goal of fostering women's rights in Afghanistan. It also supports Paul Barker's position that, "NGOs are concerned about structuring projects in a manner that promotes the representation of women and minority groups in decision-making and which promote improved equity of access to development resources in the community."

[131] Vince Crawley. 2004. "Rumsfeld Wants Soldiers Off Afghanistan Rebuilding Teams," *Army Times* 64, number 34. Pages 32-33.

funding and resources, facilitating NGO reconstruction activities and establishing a common framework for operations. It could also be responsible for developing the objective and subjective metrics for determining provincial stability. Moreover, as NATO expands throughout Afghanistan, the coalition should give thought to subordinating U.S. PRTs under ISAF command. This would permit nationwide unity of effort under centralized control and establish a clear division between counterinsurgency and reconstruction operations.

Summary

Existing PRTs appear to fall into two separate categories. ISAF PRTs are highly trained, almost exclusively manned by regular soldiers and have been proactive and evolutionary in their approach to providing regional security. In contrast, U.S. PRTs are increasingly manned by reserve and National Guard personnel and have faced considerable international criticism regarding their training proficiency, operational approach and ambiguous mandate. With ISAF poised to expand into south and southeast Afghanistan, nations wishing to establish PRTs should develop a hybrid structure and approach that meets national and ISAF expectations. Mark Sedra suggest in "The Provincial Reconstruction Team: The Future of Civil-Military Relations?" that; "A [proposed] Canadian PRT model should mirror its British equivalent in adoption of a peace-building and security approach." However, he suggests that; "It should differ by dedicating greater attention to the improvement of local governance and judicial reform ..."[132] While there are unquestionable benefits to adopting a proven national approach to regional stability, PRTs must possess a unified mission and operate within an agreed and achievable mandate. Failure to do so will challenge nationwide unity of effort, a result of which will be an inconsistent security environment throughout Afghanistan dependant upon national approaches. Moreover, nations wishing to assume the responsibility of PRT leadership should take into account structural and

---

[132] Mark Sedra. May/June 2005. "The Provincial Reconstruction Team: The Future of Civil-Military Relations?" Article in *SITREP*, A Publication of the Royal Canadian Military Institute. Official publication of the Royal Canadian Military Institute. Volume 65, Number 3.

procedural lessons learned from existing teams and give careful consideration to a practical mid-term exit strategy.

Chapter 5

Today, we lack metrics to know if we are winning or losing the global war on terror. Are we capturing, killing or deterring and dissuading more terrorists every day than the madrassas and the radical clerics are recruiting, training and deploying against us? Does the US need to fashion a broad, integrated plan to stop the next generation of terrorists? The US is putting relatively little effort into a long-range plan, but we are putting a great deal of effort into trying to stop terrorists. The cost-benefit ratio is against us! Our cost is billions against the terrorists' cost of millions.

Donald H. Rumsfeld, U.S. Secretary of Defense, 2002[133]

Review of Lessons Learned

Afghanistan is a country struggling to attain basic infrastructure, a functioning economy, civic society and a stable central government. Abject poverty, a blossoming opium trade, warlords, a collapsed public health system, militias, and a resurgent insurgency frustrate progress, especially in isolated regions. PRTs are the central component of a long-range coalition and NATO strategy to stabilize the country and facilitate reconstruction, negating the requirement for a large international peacekeeping force. However, despite the defeat of conventional Taliban and Al Qaida forces in 2002, the coalition continues to focus its primary efforts and resources on destroying the insurgent threat at the expense of PRT activities to facilitate nationwide reconstruction. To achieve long-term success, coalition and ISAF efforts should focus on facilitating reconstruction and good governance through an extensive network of robust and highly trained PRTs. Counterinsurgency operations should play a secondary and supporting role.

Existing PRTs have proven to be an unpredicted success; but they are not without their shortcomings. At the tactical level, significant variances exist in missions, mission training, focus and national expectations. At the operational level, unity of effort is routinely threatened by two

---

[133] Donald H. Rumsfeld. 16 October 2003. Rumsfeld's War on Terror Memo. Memo posted on Web site: USA Today.com. Internet. Available at: http://www.usatoday.com/news/washington/executive/rumsfeld-memo htm. Accessed 10 October 2004.

separate chains of command. Each of these areas needs to be addressed if existing and new PRTs are to play a greater role in the reconstruction of Afghanistan.

NATO is under pressure to enlarge the ISAF PRT effort into the southern and southeastern regions of Afghanistan and stands on the brink of expansion.[134] International aid organizations want ISAF to assume a greater role, as does the U.S. Secretary of Defense. In early 2004, Secretary of Defense Donald H. Rumsfeld declared emphatically that he wanted U.S. troops pulled out of the PRTs as quickly as possible, implying that ISAF must take a greater lead.[135] NATO's confirmed expansion in 2006 should allow the U.S. to scale back its 18,000-strong military presence. However, partner and non-partner countries voicing support for NATO's continuing expansion have been slow to volunteer their forces or specialist resources to meet the challenge.[136] Canada has declared its intention to establish a PRT in southern Afghanistan, as has the UK, but others have been hesitant to follow.[137] Interested nations continue to examine openly the problem. This includes those countries who staff existing PRTs in the north and northwest and who may be considering transferring their efforts to the south.

In support of the expansion of the PRT effort, national commands and NATO planners should consider the practical lessons learned from existing teams while designing optimum structures for future PRTs. Analysis of established UK, GE and U.S. PRTs has identified six

---

[134] "IRC, ICG and CARE Urge Quick Implementation of ISAF Expansion." Joint statement by Care International, the International Crisis Group, and the International Rescue Committee. Brussels, 31 October 2003. Internet. Available at: http://www.theirc.org/index.cfm/wwwID/1843. Accessed 23 February 2005.

[135] Vince Crawly. "Rumsfeld Wants Soldiers Off Afghanistan Rebuilding Teams." *Army Times* 64, number 34. 15 March 2004. Pages 32-33.

[136] Dr. Sean M. Maloney is more direct in his criticism of NATO. He states, "… the PRT expansion program, whereby NATO members have in principle agreed to accept lead-nation status for several former American OEF-run PRTs, has stalled out because of a lack of contributors." Source: "Afghanistan Four Years On: An Assessment." *Parameters*, U.S. Army War College Quarterly, Volume XXXV, No. 3. Autumn 2005. Page 30.

[137] Source: Letter to the Clerk of the Committee from the Parliamentary Relations and Devolution Department, Foreign and Commonwealth Officer, 14 March 2005. Internet. Available at: http://www.publications.parliament.uk/pa/cm200405/cmselect/cmfaff/36/36we18.htm. Accessed 9 August 2005.

essential Table of Organization and Equipment (TOE) and tactical lessons learned/recommendations. These are:

1. More female soldiers and interpreters should be included in liaison patrols to address women's needs.

2. Specialist capabilities, such as psychological operations personnel, explosive ordnance experts, information operations and human/signals intelligence personnel should be incorporated into PRT establishments.

3. PRT deployments to more insecure regions in Afghanistan require a substantially larger and more robustly equipped security force. The threat posture may require heavy weapons and a strong mobile reserve.

4. Routine and high visibility liaison patrols serve as a significant local deterrent to hostile acts and factional tension and should occur in greater frequency in areas of high threat.

5. PRTs must be adequately resourced and supported.

6. Liaison personnel should serve at least twelve consecutive months.

Ten key operational lessons/areas of concern emerge from an examination of coalition and ISAF PRTs. These are:

1. Coalition and ISAF PRTs require a unified mission and agreed on approach to establish the conditions for regional stability.

2. Coalition and ISAF PRT mandates are ambiguous and require immediate clarification and transparency to support unity of effort.

3. PRTs should be "civilianized" and "Afghanized" to restore the perception of normalcy and perhaps even lead to a reduced threat. The military should return to its primary function.

4. Each PRT should establish a dedicated intelligence cell to counter anti-government activities by focusing on counterinsurgency, crime and smuggling.

5. PRTs should develop closer working relationships with regional and militia leaders. Military or civilian liaison officers should be assigned to work with these leaders, monitoring

55

their behavior and activities and assisting them in receiving aid, medical, agricultural and other support.

6. PRTs must maximize the influence of available medical assets on the local population. As the majority of the rural areas influenced by the PRTs lack the infrastructure to meet the basic health care needs of the population, additional medical assistance (including dental and veterinarian support) is an important factor for securing the "middle ground."

7. Training for personnel deploying to PRTs must be comprehensive, structured and progressive. Individual preparation, including language and cultural training, is essential, but wide-ranging mission and team-specific training must follow. Refresher training must occur once deployed in theater.

8. PRTs should be primarily manned by regular soldiers, not reservists.

9. PRT commanders should be carefully selected. Previous operational experience, a track record of successful command and transferable skills/education are key attributes that must be included in the selection process. Selection for PRT command should be considered career enhancing.

10. Consideration should be given to establishing two separate coalition command structures in Afghanistan: counterinsurgency and reconstruction. This would address the existing friction between high-impact counterinsurgency operations and gradual reconstruction activities.

A Recommended PRT "Blueprint"

> Security is only one part of the reconstruction effort. But at the beginning it is the most important part. Good security enables the other pillars of reconstruction to maximize their efforts without interference. Effective security acts as a force multiplier to the reconstruction plan.
>
> Major Joseph F. Monroe USMC, "Afghanistan: Security Integration and Organization," 2004[138]

---

[138] Joseph F. Monroe. 2004. "Afghanistan: Security Integration and Organization." Naval War College, Newport.

Combining the pertinent lessons learned from established PRTs supports a recommended PRT "blueprint" for Afghanistan. Figure 5 shows a wire diagram of the primary components required by a PRT operating in the southern and southeastern regions of Afghanistan. The illustration does not provide a suggested level of resources or physical numbers required. PRTs should be designed to meet the individual needs of the province and population they support. Flexibility and the ability to adapt rapidly to changing priorities by restructuring will be necessary tenets for successful PRTs. Employing national "reach-back" is one way of addressing changing requirements.[139]

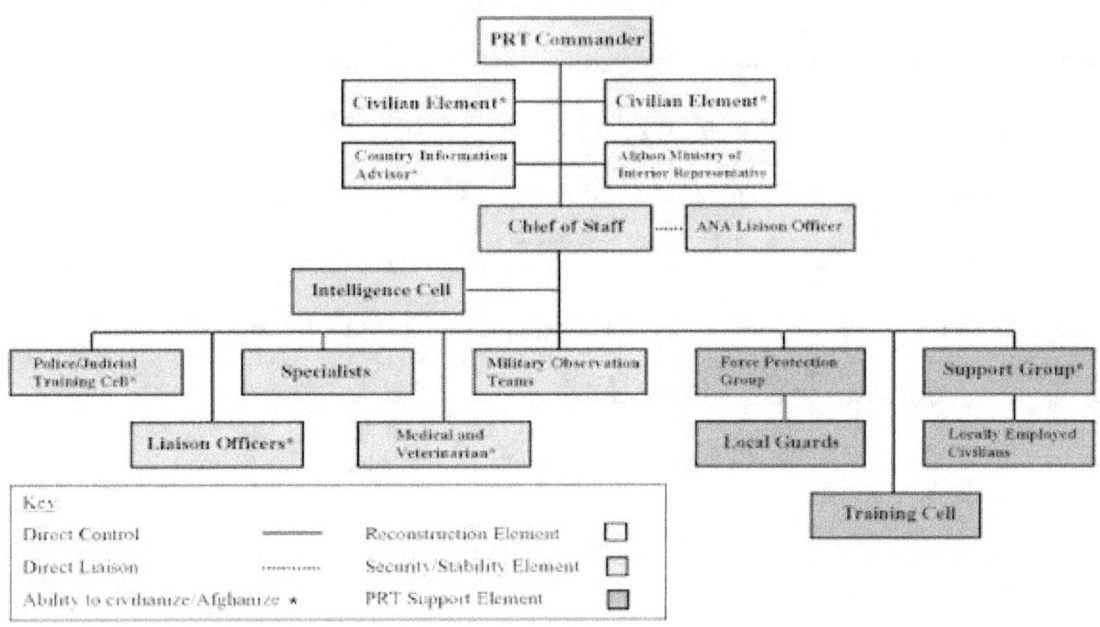

Figure 5. PRT "Blueprint" for Afghanistan.

---

[139] British Army Doctrine Publications *Land Operations*, May 2005, defines reach-back as; "Increasing use of deployable broadband communications will reduce the geographic constraints on information flow. Deployed forces can exploit this by reaching back to supporting HQs and organizations to access quality information services and advice. The development of reach-back facilities will increase functionality while reversing the trend of increasing HQ size thereby improving deployability and mobility." Page 198.

The proposed "blueprint" PRT is commanded by an experienced regular army Colonel, due to the high threat environment of the southern and southeastern regions of Afghanistan. The commander has three roles: he acts as a "first amongst equals" with his civilian counterparts in providing overarching direction for the PRT, he helps facilitate the reconstruction and development initiatives, and he has overall responsibility for maintaining regional stability. In encouraging regional reconstruction, the commander is supported by a strong civilian element. The civilian element is the lead component for facilitating reconstruction in the PRT and should increase in size as the threat decreases. The element should be sufficiently robust to help facilitate regional NGO activities and be capable of expediently drawing on national funds/resources if required. The civilian element ensures that the NGOs' resources are used effectively and are integrated into the civilian-led assistance coordination program. Incorporating a senior representative from the Afghan Ministry of the Interior is necessary for coordinating reconstruction activities with regional and national government aspirations. The commander's principal mentor is the Country Information Advisor, who should be a cultural and language expert versed in the practicalities of regional governance. In the PRT "blueprint" model, no soldiers undertake physical reconstruction activities.

The Chief of Staff (CoS), a staff college qualified lieutenant colonel or senior major, directs routine military operations, freeing the commander for liaison activities. The COS's principal role is to maintain regional security by coordinating high-visibility liaison patrols.[140] He also oversees support to institution building by monitoring direct liaison activities with local leaders and warlords, improving the proficiency of local police and coordinating combined activities with Afghan National Army units. The inclusion of an Afghan National Army (ANA) liaison officer facilitates combined planning/operations and assists with regional legitimacy. The addition of a dedicated intelligence cell, commanded by an experienced captain and subordinate

---

[140] The risks associated with isolated liaison patrols should be mitigated by the availability of a responsive air-deliverable reserve and on-call close air support.

to the CoS, provides a central function in countering insurgency activities and coordinating routine operations.

The CoS has a number of potential functional areas under his authority. The Police/Judicial Training Cell would focus on training and equipping local police forces as well as helping to reform the penal and judicial systems. Specialist capabilities, such as psychological operations personnel, explosive ordnance, information operations and human/signals intelligence personnel would be included in the PRT structure dependant upon regional necessity and availability. The CoS would also be responsible for maintaining force protection in conjunction with locally employed guards, overseeing the Support Group and ensuring regular in-theater refresher training for all personnel. The latter would be the responsibility of the Training Cell, who would also guide and support national training prior to unit rotations. Depending on the size of the force, a PRT would benefit from a logistics officer skilled in acquisition procedures.

The PRTs' principal means of maintaining regional security is through the employment of small mobile Military Observation Teams (MOTs). The number of MOTs a PRT employs will be dependant upon the threat and geographical area to be covered. MOTs act as a significant deterrent -- despite their lack of physical muscle -- to local hostilities and are a proven way of extending the reach of the PRT and government of Afghanistan into more remote areas. MOTs should include female soldiers and interpreters as well as trained medical technicians to address women's needs. They should deploy in clearly marked vehicles. The MOT's role should be to act as the "eyes and ears" of the PRT and help direct the activities of the NGOs. MOTs must not engage in physical reconstruction activities. Additionally, military or civilian liaison officers, trained in the procedures of local governance and law, should be assigned to work with regional leaders and warlords, monitoring behavior and providing a mentoring function. They must also focus their energies on facilitating the rehabilitation of local government infrastructure, an essential component of regional stability.

The challenge of establishing a PRT in the southern or southeastern region of Afghanistan is not insurmountable. U.S. PRTs have proven that stability and reconstruction operations can successfully occur in an unpredictable and often high threat environment. Drawing on lessons learned from established PRTs permits the proposal of a PRT hybrid or "blueprint" for consideration that addresses existing shortfalls of national approaches. In support of the proposed "blueprint," nations wishing to support ISAF's expansion must also give thought to how they increasingly civilianize or "Afghanize" their PRT structure. While this may challenge national regulations, such an initiative would help with perceived legitimacy, enhance local government ownership, and constitute a natural evolution of the PRT concept. Equally critical, all coalition and ISAF PRTs should operate under a unified mission, without conflicting national expectations, and possess an unambiguous, unified and transparent mandate. Moreover, all PRTs should operate within a common reporting chain that is distinct from the counterinsurgency command structure. Such a structure will enable PRTs to meet the contemporary and evolving challenges of provincial security and reconstruction in Afghanistan.

Bibliography

Books

Beckett, Ian, and John Pimlott, eds. 1985. *Armed Forces and Modern Counter-Insurgency.* London, United Kingdom: Croom Helm.

Beckett, Ian, ed. 1988. *The Roots of Counter-Insurgency: Armies and Guerrilla Warfare, 1900 - 1945.* London, United Kingdom: Blandford Press.

Briscoe, Charles, Richard Kiper, James Schroder, and Kalev Sepp. 2003. *Weapon of Choice: United States Army Special Operations Forces in Afghanistan.* Fort Leavenworth, Kansas: USA Command and General Staff College.

Cordesman, Anthony. 2004. *The Ongoing Lessons of Afghanistan: Warfighting, Intelligence, Force Transformation, and Nation Building.* Washington D.C: The Center for Strategic and International Studies.

Ewan, Martin. 2001. *Afghanistan: A Short History of Its People and Politics.* London, United Kingdom: HarperCollins Publishers.

Jalali, Ali and Lester Grau. 1995. *The Other Side of the Mountain: Mujahideen Tactics in the Soviet-Afghan War.* The United States Marine Corps Studies and Analysis Division, Quantico, Virginia (DFAR 252.227-7020 June 1995).

Kitson, Frank. 1977. *Bunch of Five.* London, United Kingdom: Faber and Faber.

Matinuddin, Kamal. 1999. *The Taliban Phenomenon: Afghanistan 1994 - 1997.* Karachi, Pakistan: Oxford University Press.

Misra, Amalendu. 2004. *Afghanistan: The Labyrinth of Violence.* Cambridge, United Kingdom: Polity Press.

Ralph, Magnus. 1998. *Afghanistan: Mullah, Marx, and Mujahid.* London, United Kingdom: HarperCollins Publishers, Inc.

Schofield, Victoria. 2003. *Afghan Frontier, Feuding and Fighting in Central Asia.* London, United Kingdom: Tauris Parke Paperbacks.

Tanner, Stephen. 2002. *Afghanistan: A Military History from Alexander the Great to the Fall of the Taliban.* New York: Da Capo Press.

Tönnies, Ferdinand. 1887. *Community and Society* (Gemeinschaft and Gesellschaft). The first English-language edition was published in 1957 by The Michigan State University Press.

Turabian, Kate L. 1996. *A Manual for Writers of Term Papers, Theses, and Dissertations.* 6th ed. Chicago: University of Chicago Press.

Weiss, Thomas G. 1999. *Military-Civilian Interactions Intervening in Humanitarian Crises.* Lanham, Maryland: Rowman and Littlefield Publishers, Inc.

Doctrine and Official Documents

Allnutt, Bruce C. 1969. "Marine Combined Action Capabilities: The Vietnam Experience." Interim Technical Report. McLean: Human Sciences Research, Inc.

U.S. Department of the Army. Field Manual 3-07 (Field Manual 100-20), *Stability Operations and Support Operations*. Washington D.C., Department of the Army, 2003.

U.S. Department of Defense. Joint Publication 3-0, *Doctrine for Joint Operations*. Washington, D.C., Department of Defense, 2001.

_____. Joint Publication 3-08, Interagency Cooperation During Joint Operations. Washington, D.C., Department of Defense, 1996.

_____. Joint Publication 5-0, *Doctrine for Planning Joint Operations*. Washington D.C., Department of Defense, 1995.

Pimlott, John. 1996. *Junior Command and Staff Course, Defense Studies, Theme C: Operations Other Than War*. Department of War Studies, Royal Military Academy Sandhurst, United Kingdom.

The White House. "National Security Strategy for Combating Terrorism." Washington D.C., 2003.

Theses and Papers

Armstrong, Bradley. 2003. "Rebuilding Afghanistan: Counterinsurgency and Reconstruction in Operation Enduring Freedom." Master of Science in Defense Analysis, Naval Postgraduate School.

Clayton, Andrew, ed. 1996. *Non-Government Organizations, Civil Society and the State: Building Democracy in Transitional Societies*. Oxford, United Kingdom: Intrac Publishers.

Donini, Antonio, Norah Niland, and Karin Wermester. 2004. *Nation-Building Unraveled? Aid, Peace and Justice in Afghanistan*. United States of America: Kumarian Press Inc.

Goodson, Larry. 2003. "Afghanistan's Long Road to Reconstruction." *Journal of Democracy*, Volume 14, Number 1 (January 2003).

Helis, James. 2003. "Nation Building, The American Way." United States Army War College, Carlisle Barracks, Pennsylvania.

Maslowsky, Robert D. 1993. "Nation-Building and the Operational Commander." United States Naval War College, Newport.

Monroe, Joseph F. 2004. "Afghanistan: Security Integration and Organization." United States Naval War College, Newport.

Perk, Scott R. 2004. "PRTs: Improving or Undermining the Security for NGOs and PVOs in Afghanistan." United States Naval War College, Newport.

Rigby, William A. 2003. "Nation Building: An Essential Army Task." U.S. Army War College, Carlisle Barracks, Pennsylvania.

Roe, Andrew M. 2005. "British Governance of the North-West Frontier (1919 to 1947): A Blueprint for Contemporary Afghanistan?" United States Army Command and General Staff College, Fort Leavenworth, Kansas.

Stapleton, Barbara J. 2003. "A British Afghan Assistance Group Briefing Paper on the Development of Joint Regional Teams in Afghanistan." The Refugee Council, January 2003.

Wardle, Russell N. 2004. "The Search for Stability: Provisional Reconstruction Teams in Afghanistan." United States Army War College, Carlisle Barracks, Pennsylvania.

Williams, Garland H. 2003. "Post Conflict Reconstruction: On the Critical Path to Long Term Peace." United States Army War College, Carlisle Barracks, Pennsylvania.

Articles in Journals and Magazines

Archer, Sarah E. "Civilian and Military Cooperation in Complex Humanitarian Operations." *Military Review* 83, no. 2 (March-April 2003): 32-41.

Crawley, Vince. 2004. "Rumsfeld Wants Soldiers Off Afghanistan Rebuilding Teams," *Army Times* 64, number 34. Pages 32-33.

Diggines, Graham. 2005. "Gurkha Road Trip." *Soldier*, Magazine of the British Army. June 2005, Volume 61/06.

Lesser, Ian, Bruce Hoffman, David Arquilla, Michele Zanini, and Brian Jenkins. 1999. "Countering the New Terrorism: Implications for Strategy," Chapter 4. Countering the New Terrorism. RAND/MR-989-AF.

Maloney, Sean M. 2005. "Afghanistan Four Years On: An Assessment." *Parameters*, U.S. Army War College Quarterly, Volume XXXV, Number 3, Autumn 2005.

McNerney, Michael J. "Stabilization and Reconstruction in Afghanistan: Are PRTs a Model or a Muddle?" *Parameters*, U.S. Army War College Quarterly, Volume XXXV, Number 4, Winter 2005-06.

Moaddel, Mansoor. 2002. *The Study of Islamic Culture and Politics: An Overview and Assessment.* Annual Review of Sociology (ABI/INFORM). Global Publishers.

Sedra, Mark. 2005. "The Provincial Reconstruction Team: The Future of Civil Military Relations?" Article in *SITREP*, A Publication of the Royal Canadian Military Institute. Official Publication of the Royal Canadian Military Institute. Volume 65, Number 3.

Articles in Newspapers and Periodicals

Chapman, Rodger, ed. 2004. *The Green Howards' Gazette*, The Regimental Magazine of The Green Howards (Alexandra, Princess of Wales's Own Yorkshire Regiment), August 2004, Volume CXII, Number 1074: Method Publishing.

Chapman, Rodger, ed. 2004. *The Green Howards' Gazette*, The Regimental Magazine of The Green Howards (Alexandra, Princess of Wales's Own Yorkshire Regiment), December 2004, Volume CXII, Number 1075: Method Publishing.

Constable, P. 2003. "Key Security Initiatives Flounder in Afghanistan Taliban Resurgent as Development, Reforms Lag." *Washington Post*. 19 September 2003, page 17.

Internet

ABCAR Policy Brief. 16 January 2003. "NGO Position Paper Concerning the Provisional Reconstruction Teams." Internet. Available at: http://www.careusa. Accessed 10 August 2005.

Afghan.com. "The Provisional Reconstruction Team (PRT) in Afghanistan and its Role in Reconstruction." Internet. Accessed 9 May 2005.

Barker, Paul. 2004. "Why PRTs Aren't the Answer." Article on-line. Available from: http://www.globalpolicy.org/ngos/aid/2004/1103prts.htm. Internet. Accessed 17 February 2005.

CARE. 2003. *CARE Calls for Critical Steps in ISAF Expansion in Afghanistan.* Article on-line. Available at: http://www.careusa.org/newsroom/pressreleases/2003/oct/10152003. Internet. Accessed 23 February 2005.

Collins, Joseph J. 2004. "US Department of Defense, NATO and the Challenges of Afghan Security." National Defense University, 28 January 2004. Internet. Available at: http://www.ndu.edu/inss/sympososia/europe2004/collinsppt.pdf. Accessed 9 August 2005.

Dempsey, Gary. 2002. "Nation Building's Newest Disguise." Article on-line. Available from: http://newfirstsearch.oclc.org. Internet. Accessed 9 October 2004.

Deutsche Welle. 2004. *Attack Raises Question over German Presence in Kunduz.* Article on-line. Available at: http://www.dw-world.de/dw/article/0,,1238505,00.html. Internet. Accessed 23 February 2005.

Donnelly, Thomas and Vance Serchuk. "Nation Building, After All." 4 April 2005. Internet. Available at: http://www.aei.org/publications/filter.all,pubID.22246/pub_detail. asap. Accessed 8 June 2005.

Foreign and Commonwealth Office Provisional Reconstruction Teams Webpage. Internet. Available at: http://www.fco.gov.uk/servlet/Front?pagename=OpenMarket/Xcelerate/ShowPage&c=Page&cid=107704746976. Accessed 17 February 2005.

ISAF Provincial Reconstruction Teams (PRTs). Internet. Available at: http://www.isaf6.eurocorps.org/article.php?article_id=37. Accessed 17 February 2005.

Jane's Executive Summary, Afghanistan. 2004. Article on-line. Available from: http://www4.janes.com. Internet. Accessed 7 October 2004.

Joint Statement by Care International, the International Crisis Group; and the International Rescue Committee. 2005. *IRC, ICG and CARE Urge Quick Implementation of ISAF Expansion.* Article on-line. Available at: http://www.rheirc.org/index.cfm/wwwID/1843. Internet. Accessed 23 February 2005.

Miles, Donna. 2004. "Terrorists Can't Compete With Provisional Reconstruction Teams." Article on-line. Available at: http://www.defenselink.mil/news/Apr2004/n042120 04_200404211.html. Internet. Accessed on 21 October 2004.

Millen, Raymond. 2005. "Afghanistan: Reconstructing a Collapsed State." Article on-line. Available at: http://www.carlisle.army.mil/ssi. Internet. Accessed 08 May 2005.

Najibullah, Farangis. 2004. "Afghanistan: Disarming The Warlords." Article on-line. Available at: http://www.dayafterindia.com/august1/afghan.html. Internet. Accessed on 29 October 2004.

NATO. 2005. "NATO in Afghanistan." Article on-line. Available at: http://www.nato.int/issues/Afghanistan/040628-factsheet.htm. Accessed 5 March 2005.

NGO/Government Dialogue on Provisional Reconstruction Teams (PRTs) in Afghanistan and the Mobilization of Humanitarian Assistance. 4 December 2003. Internet. Available at:

http://www.Peacebuild.ca/whatsnew/PRT-Dialogue-FinalReport.doc. Accessed 20 May 2005.

O'Hanlon, Michael E and Adriana Lins de Albuquerque. 2005. "Afghanistan Index: Tracking Variables of Reconstruction and Security in Post-Taliban Afghanistan." Internet. Available at: http://www.brookings.edu/afghanistanindex. Accessed 16 March 2005.

Rorke, Terri. 2003. "PRT 101: Reservist Explains Reconstruction Teams Role in Rebuilding Afghanistan." U.S. Department of Defense, *Defend American News*, July 2003. Internet. Available at: http://www.defendamerica.mil/articles/jul2003/a070303a.html. Accessed 19 February 2005.

Rumsfeld, Donald. 16 October 2003. Rumsfeld's War on Terror Memo (Memo posted on Web site: USA Today.com). Available from: http://www.usatoday.com/news/ washington/executive/rumsfeld-memo.htm. Internet. Accessed 10 October 2004.

Shape News Summary and Analysis. 2004. *Taliban Sorry for "Mistake" that Killed 16 Afghans, Says Target Was PRT.* Article on-line. Available at: http://www.globalsecurity.org/military/library/news/2004/01/mil-040107-shape02.htm. Internet. Accessed 23 February 2005.

Smith, Craig S. 2004. "NATO Runs Short of Troops to Expand Afghan Peacekeeping." Article on-line. Available at: http://proguest.umi.com/pqdweb?index=0&did=694787651&Srch. Internet. Accessed 25 January 2005.

Synovitz, Ron. 2003. *Afghanistan*: *NATO Praised for Willingness to Expand ISAF.* Article on-line. Available at: http://www.globalsecurity.org/military/library/news/2003/10/mil-031007-rferl-165134.htm. Internet. Accessed 23 February 2005.

Taylor, William B. 2004. "Testimony," U.S. Congress, Senate, Committee on Foreign Relations, Accelerate Reconstruction in Afghanistan. Washington D.C. 27 January 2004. Internet. Available at: http://www.state.gov/p/sa/rls/rm/28599.htm. Accessed 12 May 2005.

The German PRT Group. Internet. Available at: http://www.isaf6.eurocorps.org/prt.php?prt=kunduz. Accessed 14 February 2005.

Thomson, James A. 2001. *Remarks at the Opening of the 14th NATO Review Meeting,* Berlin, Germany, 19 September 2001. Article on-line. Available from: http://www.rand.org/hot/nato.html. Internet. Accessed on 06 October 2004.

USAID. 2003. "Rebuilding The Roads of Afghanistan." Article on-line. Available at: www.usaid.gov/stories/afghanistan/fp_afghan_roadparent.html. Internet. Accessed 6 December 2004.

U.S. Department of Defense. "Special Department of Defense Briefing on Provisional Reconstruction Teams in Afghanistan. Internet. Available at: http://www.defenselink.mil/transcripts/2004/tr20040217-0446.html. Accessed 25 January 2005.

Watkins, Charlotte. "PRTs." Internet. Available at: http://www.institute-for-afghan-studies.org/Contributions/Projects/Watkins-PRTs. Accessed 17 February 2005.

Briefings

Budde, Hans-Otto. 2005. "German Army Transformation." A presentation to the United States Army Command and General Staff College by the Chief of Staff of the German Army. 16 September 2005.

CARE International in Afghanistan. 2002. "Rebuilding Afghanistan: A Little Less Talk, a Lot More Action." Policy brief, October 2002.

Schwerzel, Jeffery. 2004. ISAF Overview. Headquarters ISAF Command Briefing. Kabul, Afghanistan.